Chemistry Matters!

CHEMISTRY IN ACTION

Volume 10

Allan B. Cobb

GROLIER

an imprint of

www.scholastic.com/librarypublishing

About this set

Chemistry Matters! provides an intelligent and stimulating introduction to all areas of modern chemistry as reflected in current middle school and high school curricula. This highly visual set clearly explains principles and applications using dramatic photography and annotated artwork. Carefully chosen examples make the topic fun and relevant to everyday life. Panels detail key terms, people, events, discoveries, and technologies, and include "Try This" features, in which readers are encouraged to discover principles for themselves in safe step-by-step experiments at home or school. "Chemistry in Action" boxes give everyday examples of chemical applications.

First published in 2007 by Grolier, an imprint of Scholastic Library Publishing
Old Sherman Turnpike
Danbury, Connecticut 06816

Volume ISBN 0-7172-6204-9; 978-0-7172-6204-5
Set ISBN 0-7172-6194-8; 978-0-7172-6194-9

Library of Congress Cataloging-in-Publication Data
Chemistry matters!
 v. cm.
 Includes bibliographical references and index.
 Contents: v.1. Atoms and molecules—v.2. States of matter—v.3. Chemical reactions—v.4. Energy and reactions—v.5. The periodic table—v.6. Metals and metalloids—v.7. Nonmetals—v.8. Organic chemistry—v.9. Biochemistry—v.10. Chemistry in action.
 ISBN 0-7172-6194-8 (set : alk. paper)—ISBN 0-7172-6195-6 (v.1 : alk. paper)—ISBN 0-7172-6196-4 (v.2 : alk. paper)—ISBN 0-7172-6197-2 (v.3 : alk. paper)—ISBN 0-7172-6198-0 (v.4 : alk. paper)—ISBN 0-7172-6199-9 (v.5 : alk. paper)—ISBN 0-7172-6200-6 (v.6 : alk. paper)—ISBN 0-7172-6201-4 (v.7 : alk. paper)—ISBN 0-7172-6202-2 (v.8 : alk. paper)—ISBN 0-7172-6203-0 (v.9 : alk. paper)—ISBN 0-7172-6204-9 (v.10 : alk. paper)
 1. Chemistry—Encyclopedias.
 QD4.C485 2007
 540—dc22
                              2006026209

For The Brown Reference Group plc
Project Editor: Wendy Horobin
Editors: Paul Thompson, Tim Harris,
        Tom Jackson, Susan Watt
Designer: Graham Curd
Picture Researchers: Laila Torsun, Helen Simm
Illustrators: Darren Awuah, Mark Walker
Indexer: Ann Barrett
Design Manager: Sarah Williams
Managing Editor: Bridget Giles
Production Director: Alastair Gourlay
Editorial Director: Lindsey Lowe
Children's Publisher: Anne O'Daly

Academic Consultants:
Dr. Donald Franceschetti, Dept. of Physics,
  University of Memphis
Dr. Richard Petersen, Dept. of Chemistry,
  University of Memphis

Printed and bound in Singapore.

Contents

1 Chemistry in Industry

Chemistry and chemical processes are very important in industry. Chemical processes are used to treat raw materials, such as petroleum, to extract components that people use to make many everyday things.

In no other industry is the role of chemistry more apparent than in the petrochemical industry. The petrochemical industry extracts chemicals from naturally occurring petroleum. The most obvious products of the petrochemical industry are gasoline and diesel. These are not the only fuels from the petrochemical industry. Other fuels include methane, propane, butane, kerosene, aviation fuel, and fuel oil. The petrochemical industry also produces agricultural chemicals such as herbicides, pesticides, and

Oil rigs extract oil from under the seabed. Oil is made from the decayed and compressed remains of tiny marine life-forms.

fertilizers. In addition, plastics, synthetic fibers, and asphalt are produced.

The petrochemical industry extracts such basic petrochemicals as ethylene, propylene, butadiene, benzene, isoprene, and xylenes, which are the building blocks for countless chemical products spanning the range of the plastic, rubber, and synthetic fiber industries. If you were to start making a list of where petrochemicals are used, it would include almost everything that surrounds you. Our way of life is strongly tied to the petrochemical industry.

FOSSIL FUELS

The fuels we use for transportation, energy production, and heating are often called fossil fuels. Fossil fuels, such as coal, oil, and natural gas, are made of hydrogen and carbon and are therefore called hydrocarbons. Fossil fuels occur deep underground and they form slowly over long periods of time. Coal forms from plant matter that has been compressed (squeezed) and heated from being buried so long. This compressing and heating process takes millions of years. The hard, concentrated carbon that results is coal. Oil or petroleum also forms over a long period of time. When sea creatures die, they sink to the bottom of the ocean. Over time, all these dead organisms are buried under ocean sediments. The heat and pressure cause chemical changes in the organic

material (materials containing carbon), transforming it to liquid or gaseous hydrocarbons. These hydrocarbons are lighter than rock and rise through the rock until they become trapped by a geologic structure.

Natural gas is the gaseous product of this process. The chemical name for natural gas is methane (CH_4). Methane is used as a fuel for cooking, heating, and electricity generation. Methane is an odorless gas. Therefore smelly chemicals called thiols are added to give the gas an odor. You have probably smelled the thiols if you have ever been around a gas stove with an unlit burner. The thiols are added for safety so you can tell if there is a gas leak.

▲ *The smooth red fibers are made of the plastic nylon—a synthetic fiber. Plastics are products of the petroleum industry. The rough white fibers are made of wool—a natural fiber. People can make synthetic fibers that have very different properties to those of natural fibers.*

Because all fossil fuels take very long periods of time to form, they are considered a finite, or limited, resource. Once they are used, they cannot be naturally replaced—at least not for a long time. The term used to describe finite energy resources is *nonrenewable*. By contrast, some energy sources, such as the sun or wind, are unlimited and therefore called renewable resources.

RENEWABLE ENERGY RESOURCES

Renewable energy resources are often considered "clean" energy sources because they do not produce pollutants as a waste product. When fossil fuels are burned, they release carbon dioxide, carbon monoxide, and oxides (compounds between oxygen and one other element) of sulfur and nitrogen. Renewable energy sources include solar

▲ *Wind turbines do not produce pollution but they must be sited in places where there is a steady supply of wind.*

A Closer LOOK

Solar panels

Solar panels are used to supply hot water for houses. The panels are made of a black metal plate covered with two sheets of glass. Water flows through pipes in the metal plate and is heated by the Sun. This hot water flows out of the panel and into a heat exchanger where the heat is transferred to the domestic hot water supply.

Sunlight heats the black metal plate.

heat exchanger

The hot water produced is used for heating and hot water.

glass

black metal plate

Water flowing through the plate heats up.

A pump keeps the water circulating through the panel.

Cold water enters from the main supply.

power, hydroelectric power, wind power, and geothermal power. Solar power uses the Sun's energy to generate electricity or to heat water. On a small scale, solar cells convert sunlight directly into electric energy. Solar energy works well on small applications, such as solar-powered calculators, and can be used to provide power for individual houses. However, it would be too expensive to power a large city using solar power.

Using renewable energy resources to produce power on a larger scale is more difficult than using fossil fuels. Each of the renewable energy sources has very specific requirements and will not work well everywhere. Wind and hydroelectric power generation depend on either wind or water to turn a turbine to produce electricity. For these to work, they must be done where there is steady wind or a large flow of water. Large-scale solar-power stations use solar energy to heat a liquid and turn a turbine. This requires plenty of sunlight. Geothermal energy production uses natural heat to produce steam to turn a turbine. This requires a source of geothermal energy close to the surface. Until large-scale working solutions come about, humans will continue to depend on fossil fuels.

▼ *A geothermal source of hot water can be used to supply steam. The steam can be used to power a turbine, which in turn can be used to produce electricity. In this case, hot springs in Iceland are being used to supply a town with natural hot water.*

Key Terms

- **Nonrenewable energy:** Sources of energy, such as oil and coal and other fossil fuels, that will eventually run out and cannot be replaced.
- **Renewable energy:** Unlimited sources of energy, such as sunlight and wind.

TRY THIS

Solar oven

You know that the Sun is hot but did you know that you can actually cook with solar energy? All you need to do is build a solar oven that concentrates the Sun's energy onto some food.

Materials: 1 large pizza box, 1 small pizza box, cardboard, old newspapers, aluminum foil, tape, black construction paper, 1 drinking straw, modeling clay, scissors, heavyweight clear plastic or a thin sheet of glass, marshmallows

1. Line the bottom of the large pizza box with crumpled newspaper. Place the small box in the large box and fill the space between them with more crumpled newspaper. Cut cardboard to fit between the two boxes and secure with tape.

2. Draw a square on top of the small box 1 inch (2.5 cm) from the edges. Cut three sides of this square to make a lid. Line the sides of the small box and the underside of the flap with aluminum foil. Make sure the shiny side of the foil is uppermost. Line the bottom of the small box with black paper.

3. Prop up the lid with a straw and modeling clay. Lay the sheet of plastic or glass over the square hole. Take the pizza oven out into the sun and place marshmallows on the sheet of plastic or glass. Make sure the sun is shining on the foil.

4. Wait for the marshmallows to warm up.

small pizza box

crumpled newspaper

12,5"

large pizza box

▲ *Make sure there is plenty of crumpled newspaper between the two boxes. This will help retain heat in the small box.*

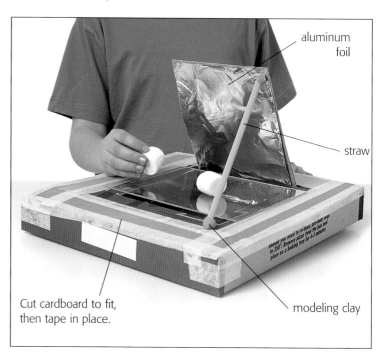

aluminum foil

straw

Cut cardboard to fit, then tape in place.

modeling clay

▲ *The oven will work best in plenty of strong sunlight.*

CRUDE OIL TO PETROCHEMICALS

Geologists use detailed information about the geology of an area to locate where oil is found. When they find a likely spot, an oil well is drilled. If they are lucky, they find oil where they drilled and will be able to pump it from the ground. When petroleum is pumped out of the ground, it is called crude oil. Before it can be used, it must be processed. Crude oil can be almost clear to very thick and black to a waxy solid. Crude oil is made up of differing percentages of hydrocarbons such as

A Closer LOOK

Petroleum traps

Petroleum moves through reservoir rock until it reaches a geologic structure that prevents it from moving farther. When this happens, the petroleum is trapped and can collect. When geologists look for places to drill, they look for geologic structures that can cause petroleum to collect. If they are lucky, they find a place where enough oil has collected that it is economically feasible to drill a well and remove the oil. There are many different kinds of traps and this illustration shows one of the simplest.

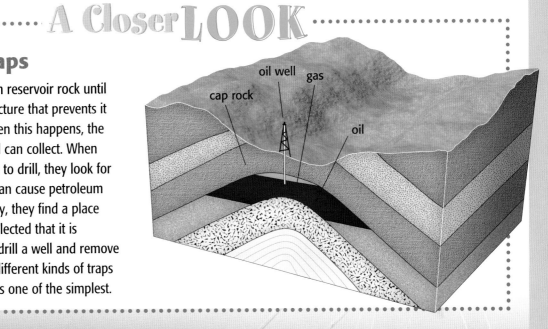

▼ The Trans-Alaska pipeline carries crude oil across Alaska over a distance of 800 miles (1,280 km) from the North Slope of Alaska to the coastal town of Valdez. The pipeline crosses 800 rivers and streams and has 11 pumping stations.

A Closer LOOK

Fractional distillation

This illustration shows a fractional distillation column used to separate crude oil into its various components.

Crude oil is first super-heated with steam and turned into a gas. Then it is sent into the fractional distillation tower. As the super-heated crude oil moves up in the tower, it cools, and the different components condense and are collected.

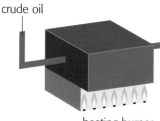

fractional distillation tower

petroleum gas, less than 40°C

gasoline, 40–200°C

kerosene, 200–250°C

heating oil, 250–300°C

lubricating oil, 300–370°C

crude oil

heating burner

residue, asphalt

FRACTIONAL DISTILLATION

Each component of crude oil has a different boiling point. By heating the oil to these different boiling points, each hydrocarbon can be extracted as a gas. This process is called fractional distillation. The lightest components, starting with methane, boil off first. As the temperature increases, heavier components boil off and are collected. Through this simple process, crude oil is separated into its different components, or fractions.

The amount produced of specific chemicals such as gasoline can be increased using a conversion process. A conversion process changes less valuable fractions from distillation into more valuable products. These conversion processes include thermal cracking, catalytic cracking, and polymerization, which is the method that produces plastics.

CRACKING

Cracking petroleum fractions involves heat, pressure, and time. Thermal cracking exposes a fraction to high temperature and pressure that causes some of the atoms to split off and form different molecules. Catalytic cracking has the same outcome only it depends on the presence of substances called catalysts, which speed up reactions. Both of these processes require precise control of temperature and pressure.

After fractional distillation and cracking, the different fractions are then treated to remove impurities. The unwanted components are removed and then each fraction is cooled and blended

paraffins, aromatics, naphthenes, alkanes, alkenes, and alkynes (*see* vol. 8). Crude oil actually contains hundreds of different hydrocarbons. To be useful, the crude oil needs to be separated into its individual components.

Key Terms

- **Cracking:** Process by which products of fractional distillation are broken down into simpler hydrocarbons.
- **Fractional distillation:** Process of heating crude oil to separate it into different components.

with other fractions to create specific end products. It is the blending process that creates the different grades of gasoline and diesel, different types and weights of lubricating oils, various grades of jet fuel, and the raw materials for making plastics.

PLASTICS

One of the biggest uses of petrochemicals is in the plastics industry. Plastics are commonly used because they have very desirable properties (*see* vol. 8: pp. 56–65). Plastics can be shaped, molded, cast, and worked into many different forms. Different plastics also have different properties. Some are soft and pliable while others are hard and rigid.

Plastics are polymers. Polymers are long chains of atoms. The long chains are made of repeating collections of atoms called monomers. Most monomers are made of carbon but some contain nitrogen, oxygen, chlorine, or sulfur. The composition of the monomer also affects the properties of the polymer.

▲ Plastics are made from petrochemicals. Kayaks are an example of something once made of natural materials (wood and animal skin) that are now commonly made of plastic.

Ethene

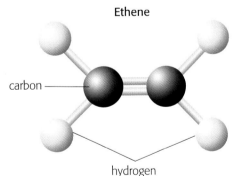

carbon

hydrogen

◀ The monomer ethene is made of two carbon and four hydrogen atoms.

◀ The plastic polyethylene is made by connecting many ethene molecules, forming a long chain. Here, only a small portion of the chain is shown. In reality it would be much longer.

Polyethylene hydrogen

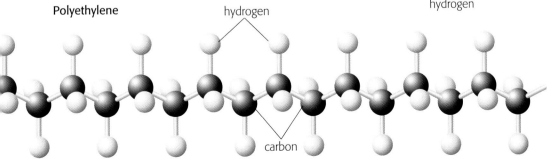

carbon

Nylon is a plastic and is made of carbon, hydrogen, nitrogen, and oxygen. The U.S. chemical company DuPont introduced nylon to the public at the 1939 World's Fair in New York City. Nylon is a long, flexible, and strong synthetic fiber. Early uses of nylon were for bristles in toothbrushes and to replace silk in stockings. Today it is used for making products such as fabrics and gears.

Another common plastic is synthetic rubber. Natural rubber comes from the sap of rubber trees. As cars became more common, the need for rubber for tires was greater than the rubber plantations could supply. In 1935, a German chemist was the first to make a synthetic substitute. Today, the amount of synthetic rubber produced is far greater than the amount of natural rubber that was ever produced.

▷ *Strings for classical guitars are commonly made of nylon, which is strong and durable. Nylon fibers are also used to make clothes, rope, and the fabric for parachutes.*

Chemistry in Action

Teflon

Teflon is a polymer of fluorine and ethylene (ethene) called polytetrafluorethylene (PTFE). Roy J. Plunkett (1910–1994), a DuPont chemist, discovered Teflon when he was working on finding a new refrigerant in 1938. The nonstick properties of Teflon were realized and it was used for several different applications. One of the first successful applications was for coating cookware. Teflon-coated cookware has amazing nonstick properties. Teflon produces less friction than any other solid so it is also useful in applications where surfaces slide on each other. Teflon may be found in bearings and gears where smooth sliding surfaces are important.

PETE   HDPE   V   LDPE   PP   PS   OTHER

RECYCLING PLASTICS

Plastics are very durable and break down very slowly. These characteristics make plastics very useful but also create problems. After a plastic product is used and discarded, it may take several hundred years for it to decay. A solution to this problem is to recycle plastics. Today, plastics are marked with a recycle code. This way, similar plastics can be grouped and recycled together. Recycling plastic not only reduces the amount of petrochemicals needed for production, but it reduces the amount of waste in landfills.

◭ *Recycling symbols are used to identify different types of plastics so they can be easily separated and recycled. From left to right these plastics are, polyethylene terephthalate, high-density polyethylene, polyvinyl chloride, low-density polyethylene, polypropylene, polystyrene, and other plastics.*

◭ *These plastic bottles, made of polyethylene terephthalate (PETE), have been sorted for recycling.*

CHEMICAL ENGINEERING

Chemical engineering is the field of designing chemical processes for large-scale manufacturing applications. This field is only a little more than 100 years old. Before chemical engineering, chemical processes were done in batches. This system often resulted in inconsistent products. The quality of the results was variable and could not be relied on from batch to batch. The need to standardize chemical processes to produce uniform results gave rise to the science of chemical engineering.

The goal of chemical engineering is to make the unit processes controlled and cost effective. This ensures that the results are both uniform and

George Davis, father of chemical engineering

George Davis (1850–1906) was an alkali inspector in England. His job was to inspect alkali processing facilities and monitor them for compliance with pollution regulations. His job took him through many different plants using many different processes. Some of these plants were engineering marvels of their time. However, there were still problems with the chemical processes. Davis saw a need to combine traditional engineering practices and chemistry to create a field of chemical engineering. In 1887, he presented a series of lectures on the subject of chemical engineering. Soon after, the Massachusetts Institute of Technology (MIT) developed the first college course of study in chemical engineering.

Haber process

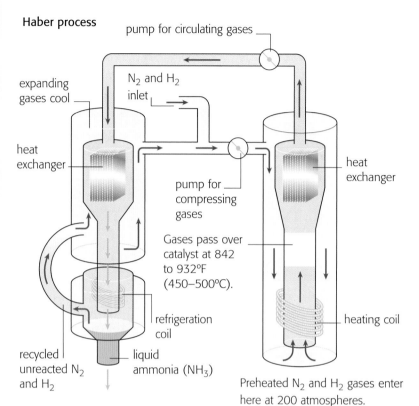

pump for circulating gases

N₂ and H₂ inlet

expanding gases cool

heat exchanger

pump for compressing gases

Gases pass over catalyst at 842 to 932°F (450–500°C).

refrigeration coil

recycled unreacted N₂ and H₂

liquid ammonia (NH₃)

heat exchanger

heating coil

Preheated N₂ and H₂ gases enter here at 200 atmospheres.

◄ *The Haber process uses nitrogen and hydrogen to make ammonia. Nitrogen and hydrogen are first mixed and then compressed. The compressed mixture is heated and passed over a catalyst that speeds up the reaction. The resulting gas is a mixture of ammonia (NH₃), hydrogen, and nitrogen.*

HABER PROCESS

The Haber process is the reaction of nitrogen and hydrogen to produce ammonia. On paper, this is a very simple reaction:

$$N_2(g) + 3H_2(g) \rightarrow 2NH_3(g)$$

However, this reaction takes place over an iron catalyst—a substance that speeds up reactions. The reaction also takes place at high pressure and temperature. In the products of this process, only 10 to 20 percent is ammonia. German chemist Fritz Haber (1868–1934) patented this process in

produced as cheaply as possible. To meet these goals, chemical engineers learn the details of the chemical reactions and design the components needed for the reactions.

FROM LABORATORY TO INDUSTRY

Producing chemicals in industrial settings is much different from working in a laboratory. In a laboratory, the reaction vessels and quantities of chemicals are often quite small. In industry, the reactions must take place on a much larger scale to produce enough chemicals to make the process cost effective. There are many different industrial processes that are used every day. Four important industrial processes are the Haber process, the Frasch process, the contact process, and the Solvay process.

▼ *The Frasch process is used to extract sulfur from natural underground deposits.*

1908. Today, this process is used to make anhydrous ammonia (ammonia that is not dissolved in water), ammonium nitrate (NH_4NO_3), and urea (CON_2H_4) for the fertilizer industry.

FRASCH PROCESS

Sulfur is an important chemical used in a wide variety of products ranging from explosives to fertilizers. It is also used to make sulfuric acid, which is used in many other chemical processes. The Frasch process is one of the ways sulfur is obtained. In 1867, sulfur deposits were found under quicksand in Texas and Louisiana. An American chemist named Herman Frasch (1851–1914) devised a way to easily mine the sulfur.

Using this process, a hole is drilled into the underground sulfur deposit. A large

▼ *The contact process is used to manufacture sulfuric acid (H_2SO_4).*
1. First sulfur dioxide (SO_2) gas is formed by burning dry sulfur.
2. At a temperature around 842°F (450°C), the hot gas reacts with oxygen to form sulfur trioxide, SO_3.
3. The sulfur trioxide is then dissolved in concentrated sulfuric acid to form oleum ($H_2S_2O_7$).
4. This is then diluted with water to produce sulfuric acid.

pipe containing smaller pipes is placed in the hole. Steam is pumped into the sulfur deposit through some of the pipes. The steam heats up the sulfur until it melts. Compressed air is forced down some of the pipes, and the molten sulfur flows out through the pipes. On reaching the surface, the sulfur turns back into a solid. This process yields sulfur that is about 99 percent pure.

CONTACT PROCESS

Highly concentrated sulfuric acid is used in many industrial reactions. British vinegar merchant Peregrine Phillips patented the contact process in 1831.

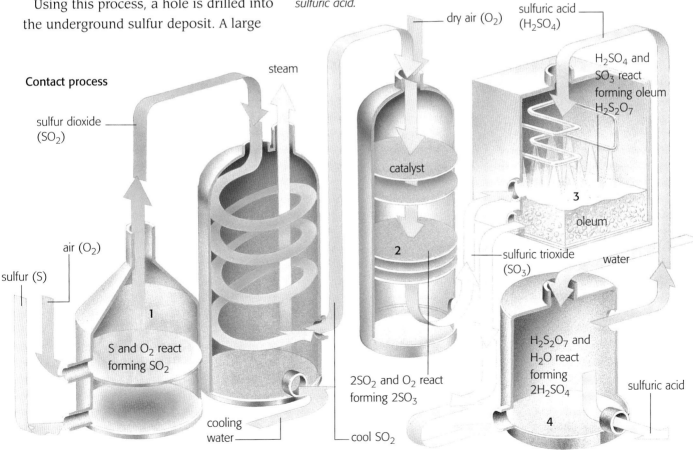

Contact process

sulfur dioxide (SO_2)

steam

air (O_2)

sulfur (S)

1

S and O_2 react forming SO_2

cooling water

cool SO_2

$2SO_2$ and O_2 react forming $2SO_3$

catalyst

2

dry air (O_2)

sulfuric acid (H_2SO_4)

H_2SO_4 and SO_3 react forming oleum $H_2S_2O_7$

3

oleum

sulfuric trioxide (SO_3)

water

$H_2S_2O_7$ and H_2O react forming $2H_2SO_4$

4

sulfuric acid

The contact process was more economical than other methods used to produce sulfuric acid and it is still used today. Sulfur dioxide (SO_2) is produced under 200 atmospheres (atm) of pressure and 842 degrees Fahrenheit (842°F; 450°C). Then, the sulfur dioxide undergoes a process called catalytic oxidation and becomes sulfur trioxide (SO_3). This happens in the presence of a catalyst called vanadium oxide. The sulfur trioxide is added to concentrated sulfuric acid (H_2SO_4) to form a liquid called oleum ($H_2S_2O_7$). Water is then added to the oleum to make sulfuric acid.

SOLVAY PROCESS

The Solvay process is the industrial process used to produce soda ash (sodium carbonate, Na_2CO_3). A Belgian chemist named Ernest Solvay (1838–1932) developed this process in 1861.

The Solvay process produces sodium carbonate from sodium chloride (NaCl) and calcium carbonate ($CaCO_3$). The calcium carbonate is dissolved in a brine solution (salty water) with ammonia. Carbon dioxide is bubbled through the brine solution, and sodium bicarbonate precipitates out (settles out). Heating the sodium bicarbonate decomposes it (breaks it down) into sodium carbonate and carbon dioxide.

About half of the sodium carbonate is used in glassmaking. The rest is used in making soaps and detergents, making paper, and other industrial applications. The Solvay process is used worldwide, except in the United States. Sodium carbonate deposits in Wyoming provide a cheaper source that is easily mined.

▼ Sodium carbonate is manufactured using the Solvay process. Calcium carbonate ($CaCO_3$) is dissolved in brine (1), which is also saturated with ammonia, NH_3 (2). Carbon dioxide (CO_2) is bubbled through the mixture in a reaction tower (3), resulting in sodium bicarbonate, $NaHCO_3$ (4), or baking soda. This is then heated (5) producing sodium carbonate (Na_2CO_3) and carbon dioxide.

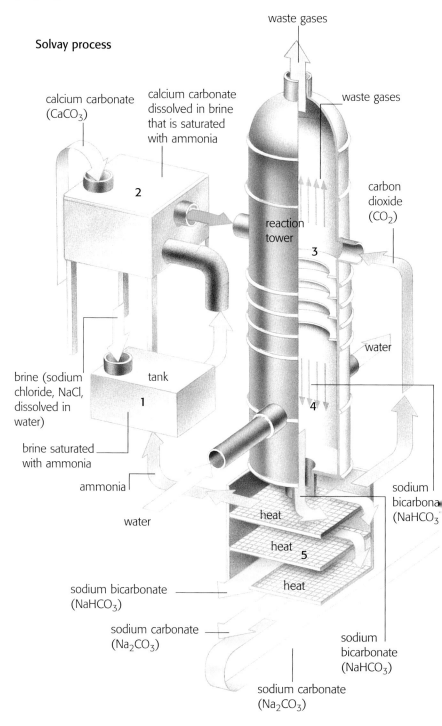

Solvay process

Chemistry in Action

Glassmaking

The chemistry of glassmaking has remained almost unchanged for more than 3,500 years. The main component of glass is silica. The common source of silica is silicon dioxide, or sand. Silica has a melting point of about 3,632 degrees Fahrenheit (3,632°F; 2,000°C). Adding about 18 percent sodium carbonate lowers the melting point to 1,832°F (1,000°C). The addition of calcium carbonate makes the glass more resistant to chemical weathering. Glass is melted and then poured into different shapes. The glass can then be further worked to make a variety of glass products.

▲ A technician supervises the manufacture of a large glass tube. Glass is an incredibly versatile material and when hot can be molded into practically any shape.

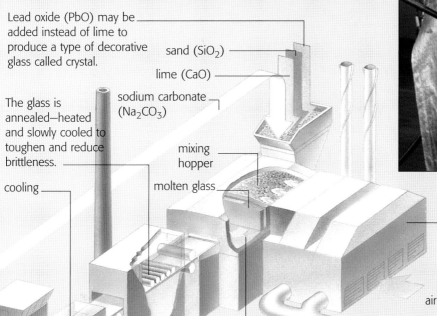

Lead oxide (PbO) may be added instead of lime to produce a type of decorative glass called crystal.

sand (SiO_2)

lime (CaO)

sodium carbonate (Na_2CO_3)

The glass is annealed—heated and slowly cooled to toughen and reduce brittleness.

cooling

mixing hopper

molten glass

oil-fired furnace

air

fuel oil

molten tin

cutting

finished glass

▲ Sodium carbonate is important in the manufacture of glass. The main constituent of glass is sand (SiO_2), which is mixed with lead, lime, and sodium carbonate. This mixture is melted to produce glass.

FERTILIZERS

Fertilizers are classified as either organic or inorganic. Organic fertilizers come from natural sources such as manure, urine, peat, seaweed, guano (seabird or bat excrement), or mineral deposits.

Chemistry in Action

Choosing the right fertilizer

The NPK number tells you what the fertilizer contains. You might think that choosing a fertilizer with the highest number in each category is best, but this might not be the case. Different plants have different requirements for each of these three elements. Here is a general guideline of what different plants need.

General purpose fertilizer—designed to provide basic nutrients for any plant but best for trees and shrubs.

Lawn fertilizer—usually has more nitrogen, which grass needs for healthy growth.

Flower garden fertilizer—usually has a bit more phosphorus to encourage blossoms.

Vegetable garden fertilizer—usually has a higher percentage of all three elements since vegetables are often closely planted and therefore need more food.

materials. For example the Haber process is responsible for making ammonia used in inorganic fertilizers. In 2004, 120 million tons (109 million metric tons) of ammonia were produced worldwide and more than 80 percent of it was used as fertilizer. Anhydrous ammonia is either directly added to the soil or used in the production of an NPK fertilizer.

Crops are grown repeatedly on a piece of land. Some farming practices allow the field to remain fallow, or unplanted, for a growing season or two. The fallow land may even be planted with a crop that actually enhances the amount of nutrients in the soil. Then before planting a crop, the plants are turned into the soil and allowed to decompose to release nutrients.

Organic fertilizers supply nitrogen (N), phosphorus (P), and potassium (K) for plants. They also contain many trace elements used by plants. Inorganic fertilizers are synthesized commercially. Inorganic fertilizers usually only contain nitrogen, phosphorus, and potassium. They are labeled with an NPK number that indicates the amount of each of these elements. They seldom have any of the trace elements needed by plants. This means that the trace elements already present in the soil are depleted over time.

Inorganic fertilizers rely on various chemical processes for their raw

▶ *Flowering plants need phosphorus to produce a good show of blooms. Gardeners add this vital nutrient in the form of a fertilizer that has been specially formulated to encourage flowering.*

TRY THIS

Electrolysis of water

In this activity, you will have a chance to perform electrolysis. In contrast to the chlor-alkali process (*see* p. 20), which uses brine to produce chlorine gas, hydrogen gas, and sodium hydroxide, you will use water and split it into hydrogen and oxygen.

Materials: large glass beaker or jar, two test tubes or clear vials, 6-volt battery, two 8–inch (20–cm) pieces of wire, water, baking soda

1. Mix two tablespoons of baking soda in two cups of water. Stir until the baking soda has dissolved. Then pour about 1 cup of the solution into a beaker or jar.

2. Place one of the stripped ends of each wire into the beaker or jar.

3. Fill each test tube to the top with the leftover solution, then hold your finger over the open end as you immerse it upside-down in the beaker of solution. Position one tube over the end of each wire.

▼ When the wires are connected to the battery, the top of the inverted test tubes begins to fill with gas. One fills with oxygen and the other with hydrogen.

4. Connect the wires to the batteries and observe what happens at the tip of each wire in the solution. Let the reaction continue for at least five minutes.

You should notice a difference in the levels of gases in the two tubes. Why do you think there is a difference? (HINT: water has two hydrogen atoms for every oxygen atom.)

Answer There should be more hydrogen since water contains twice as many hydrogen atoms as oxygen atoms.

It is important to carefully monitor and control the condition of the soil for crops. The excessive use of fertilizer can cause environmental problems. Excess fertilizer can run off the fields and get into waterways, stimulating growth of aquatic plants and algae that can choke waterways and kill fish.

CHLOR-ALKALI PROCESS
The chlor-alkali process is the electrolysis of sodium chloride (NaCl) dissolved in water to produce chlorine gas, hydrogen gas, and sodium hydroxide. These products are useful in different industrial processes. The chlor-alkali process replaced the

previous production method because it used mercury. The chlor-alkali process does not use mercury and it produces three usable products: chlorine (Cl), hydrogen (H), and sodium hydroxide (NaOH). These products are produced in the following reaction:

$$2NaCl + 2H_2O \rightarrow Cl_2 + H_2 + 2NaOH$$

Chlorine gas is used in many different applications. One of the most widespread is to disinfect water. It is used in water-treatment plants to kill microorganisms and bacteria in drinking water. It is very effective and preferable to other methods used to disinfect municipal water. Chlorine is also widely used for disinfecting swimming pools.

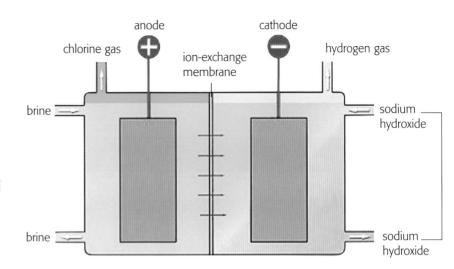

▲ The chlor-alkali process uses an electric current passed through brine (blue) to produce chlorine, hydrogen, and sodium hydroxide. Chlorine gas collects at the anode (positive electrode), and hydrogen gas collects at the cathode (negative electrode). Sodium hydroxide (pink) is pumped in and out of the cell, but more leaves than is pumped in so there is an overall net gain.

Tools and Techniques

Chemical efficiency

Industrial chemical processes must be efficient—they must produce the maximum amount of product with the least waste. The efficiency of a chemical process is calculated with the following equation:

% efficiency = (actual yield)/(theoretical yield) x 100

This is the simplest method for determining efficiency. A process that is 90 percent efficient is better than one that is 20 percent efficient. However, there are also other factors to consider. The lower efficiency reaction may be more cost-effective (cheapest overall) because it requires less energy, creates fewer by-products, or requires fewer chemicals. Calculating the most cost-effective process often becomes very complicated.

Another common use for chlorine is chlorine bleach—an additive for washing clothes. Chlorine is also used widely in paper product production, antiseptics, dyestuffs, food, insecticides, paints, petroleum products, plastics, medicines, textiles, solvents, and many other consumer products.

Sodium hydroxide is used in the soap-making process as well as in food processing. In food processing, it is used in the production of soft drinks, pretzels, ice cream, and chocolate, and also in the washing of fruits and vegetables. Sodium hydroxide is also used as a drain cleaner because it breaks down the complex proteins often found in substances that block drains. Because sodium hydroxide breaks down bonds, it is also used to produce biodiesel, a synthetic fuel made from vegetable oil.

◄ *Chemists perform an analysis on a chemical sample. Analytical chemistry is essential for the smooth running of chemical industries. By analyzing the products of various processes, chemists can assess whether the processes are running correctly and efficiently.*

ANALYTICAL CHEMISTRY

There will always be a need for chemists in industry. Chemical engineers design the processes that run the industry but chemists check the products forming at the beginning, middle, and end of the processes to make sure they are running properly. Almost every industrial setting that uses chemical processes has chemists monitoring their progress. Depending on the process, a chemist will use a particular analytical method.

Analytical chemistry is the chemical analysis of materials to gain an understanding of properties such as composition, structure, function, and concentration. Analytical chemists use a variety of instruments and methods to accurately gather this information. In spectroscopic analysis, chemists analyze the electromagnetic waves, such as light and radio waves, given off by a sample (*see* vol. 5: p. 14). In electrochemical analysis, devices are used that generate an electric response in certain chemicals. In mass analysis, chemists use machines called mass spectrometers to measure the masses of the individual elements in a substance (*see* vol. 1: p. 33). In thermal analysis, the physical and chemical properties of a material are studied as it changes temperature.

The data obtained using these methods is then analyzed and compared with known standards for the materials and processes involved. The chemist then evaluates the information and prepares a report. A chemical engineer reviews the report and makes changes in the processes if necessary.

See Also ...
Carbon Chains,
Vol. 8: pp. 18–29.
Catalysts,
Vol. 4: pp. 56–65.

2 Metals and Metallurgy

One of the largest industries worldwide is the extraction and processing of metals. People have to extract metals from rock and put them through a series of chemical and physical processes before the metals can be used.

Metals are used in many different products. Metals are useful because they can be bent, pounded, drawn, or cast into shapes. Different metals have different properties and these properties determine how it is used. Aluminum is a metal used in various applications. Aluminum is used in engine parts, the skin and structure of airplanes, in soda cans, and as aluminum foil. Throughout this chapter, you will learn more about metals—where they come from, their properties, and how they are used.

Metals can be bent and shaped to form many useful objects, such as cars, that need a strong casing.

PROSPECTING FOR MINERALS

Few metals are found as raw metals in their natural state. Most metals undergo chemical reactions with other elements and occur as minerals. Minerals are crystalline chemical compounds. Because the metal is mixed with other elements, some of its chemical properties may have changed, so finding metals can be difficult. The act of trying to find metals is called prospecting. Prospecting is done using a number of techniques.

In the past, prospectors used methods based on superstition or chance. Sometimes they used tools such as divining rods to try to locate minerals. While these methods occasionally worked, finding a deposit was more often a lucky coincidence. Today, prospecting for minerals is far more scientific.

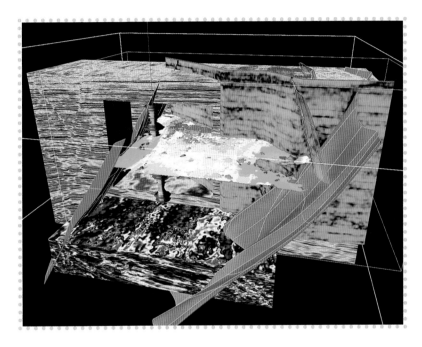

Key Terms

- **Deposit:** A mineral vein or ore inside another rock.
- **Geologist:** Scientist who studies rocks and minerals.
- **Metallurgy:** The science and technology of metals, including methods of extraction and use.
- **Seismic survey:** A method of determining the structure of underground rock formations by measuring the vibrations produced by test explosions.

Modern prospecting uses a variety of methods such as extensive surface and subsurface rock sample collection, measuring variations in the magnetic or gravitational fields, or seismic surveys. The data collected is carefully analyzed to locate mineral sources.

Geologists use a number of different tools to help with prospecting. The tools a geologist uses depend on the minerals he or she is seeking. If a geologist is prospecting for radioactive minerals, a Geiger counter is used to detect radiation. Some minerals fluoresce (glow) under ultraviolet light, so an ultraviolet light is another important tool.

Geologists also depend on chemistry when prospecting. Important minerals are often associated with certain

▲ Seismic probes have been used to gather data that has produced this computer-generated map of underground rock formations. The colors represent different rock types. Some of these structures would not be visible from the surface, which makes this tool extremely useful in locating mineral deposits.

A Closer LOOK

Streak test

One of the quick tests to identify a mineral is called the streak test. A streak plate is a piece of unglazed porcelain. When a mineral is rubbed on the streak plate, a mark is left on the surface. The color of the mark may not be the same as the original mineral sample but each mineral always leaves a unique streak color. A geologist uses the streak color to help determine the identity of a particular mineral.

▶ *Iron pyrite, or fool's gold, is a sulfide of iron. Although it is mainly used as a source of iron and sulfur, there may also be small quantities of actual gold mixed with the pyrite.*

▼ *This rock face shows several seams of reddish brown iron ore running diagonally through it. The ore has to be processed to release the pure metal.*

elements. The elements associated with the desired minerals are called pathfinder elements. For example, gold deposits are often associated with antimony and arsenic. A geologist can have rock samples analyzed for antimony and arsenic and hopefully the data will lead the geologist to a body of gold ore.

MINING AND ORE EXTRACTION

Mining is the process by which valuable minerals are removed from the ground. The valuable mineral may be in an ore body, a vein, or a seam. An ore body is a volume of rock that contains a small amount of the mineral spread throughout the rock. A vein is formed when a concentrated molten mineral fills a crack in the surrounding rock and cools. A seam is an entire layer of rock that contains a concentrated mineral. A seam is usually larger and more extensive than a vein.

The type of mining carried out depends on how and where the mineral occurs.

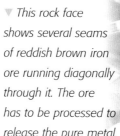

▲ *Red iron ore has been removed from the ground by digging it out, forming an open pit.*

mining is relatively inexpensive but can create environmental problems that may be difficult to solve.

Surface mining is used to remove a variety of different minerals. Coal, oil sands, metals, and other commercially useful minerals are all extracted by surface mining. Often, huge quantities of rock have to be stripped away first to reach the minerals. Consequently, the machinery used in surface mining is also quite large. Surface mining is expensive and is usually only cost effective when done on a large scale.

If the mineral is found at or close to the surface, surface mining is carried out. Surface, or open pit, mining requires a large area because the entire surface is dug up, forming an open pit. Surface

If the minerals are located deep underground, surface mining is not practical. In such cases, subsurface or

Chemistry in Action

Acid mine drainage

Metal mines often result in acid mine drainage. Metals, such as iron, zinc, copper, and nickel, are usually found in minerals as sulfides. When exposed to air, these metal sulfides break down into metal ions and sulfide. Bacteria metabolize the sulfides and produce sulfuric acid. The sulfuric acid runs off from the mine and contaminates local watercourses with both acids and heavy metals.

▶ *This river is polluted with acid from a copper mine upstream. The acid has killed all life in the river.*

underground mining is used. Subsurface mining requires special equipment to work underground. The work can be dangerous because of rock collapses or poisonous gases. Subsurface mining often has less environmental impact than surface mining.

Subsurface mining faces many problems. First, the equipment and the people who run the equipment must be able to travel deep underground. Ventilation must be installed to provide fresh air, and power is needed for lighting and the equipment. All materials mined must be transported from the mine to the surface. That includes both the minerals being mined and the surrounding rock that is also mined. Working in such mines is always dangerous.

REFINING ORES AND MINERALS

After the minerals are removed from the ground by mining, they must be processed to extract the important minerals or elements. The method of extraction used will depend on the chemical and physical properties of the minerals. Metals are often removed from ores by reducing the metals in the ore. Reducing metals involves reacting the ore so that the metal separates out. The two most common methods used are chemical and electrolytic.

Chemical methods of reducing metal ores involve smelting the ore with a reducing agent such as coke (carbon derived from coal) or charcoal. The molten metal is then separated from the waste, or slag. This process is used for

▲ *Mining coal deep underground is a hazardous business. The coal seam must be carefully cut to avoid the layers of rock above from collapsing into the tunnel.*

A Closer LOOK

Aluminum processing

The Hall–Héroult process was discovered in 1886. It was the first method discovered to smelt aluminum metal from its aluminum oxide ore. Aluminum oxide is melted with cryolite (Na_3AlF_6) and an electric current of 150,000 amperes at a voltage of 3 to 5 volts is passed through the molten metal. Aluminum processing consumes huge amounts of electricity and the processing plants are usually found close to cheap sources of power such as hydroelectric plants. Recycling aluminum requires only about 5 percent of the power needed to produce new aluminum.

▲ These pipes supply the plant at the center of the picture with water. The water is used to generate electricity to extract aluminum by electrolysis.

▼ These shallow ponds are being used to evaporate a solution containing potash, which is a mixture of potassium compounds. Water is pumped into potash deposits underground and the dissolved potash is brought back to the surface to dry out.

metals such as iron and copper. The resulting molten metal is very pure and ready to be used in other processes.

Electrolytic methods involve passing electric current through the mineral. This process is used to extract metals from salts (*see* vol. 3: pp. 56–57). The metal salt must be either molten or in an aqueous solution (dissolved in water) form. The electric current is passed through the molten or dissolved minerals and metal begins to plate one of the electrodes. This process is used for the production of aluminum and nickel.

A variety of other methods are also used to extract minerals. Most of these methods depend on the physical properties of the minerals. One method is solvent extraction, in which a solvent is used to dissolve the mineral from the other material (*see* box p. 29). The

solvent used is typically an acid. It is useful for extracting minerals that are carbonate compounds (containing CO_3).

Another method is called froth flotation. Froth flotation takes advantage of the hydrophobic character of many minerals. Hydrophobic minerals are repelled by water so they will be found in the froth on top of a water solution. Hydrophilic minerals are attracted to the water and are found in the water portion. This method is used with some types of oxide and sulfide minerals.

Mechanical separation is also a method used to separate minerals. Some minerals can be separated by gravity separation. This method separates minerals based on their relative densities—heavy minerals sink, lighter ones float. Electrostatic separation uses an electric charge to attract some minerals. Other minerals can be separated by using strong magnets to attract magnetic particles.

USES OF METALS

To a chemist a metal is any element that readily forms a positive ion. (An ion is an atom that has gained an electrical charge through gain or loss of electrons.) However, when discussing metals related

TRY THIS

Separating mixtures

Minerals can be separated by their physical properties. This quick activity show you how it is done.

Materials: sand, salt, sawdust, water

1. Mix the sand, salt, and sawdust together.

2. This mixture can be easily separated using water. Add water and watch the sawdust float. Carefully remove the sawdust from the top of the water.

3. Salt is soluble in water but the sand is not. So, if you pour the water off the sand, you can leave the water to evaporate (turn to vapor) in the sun and recover the salt.

Using these simple techniques, the three components of the mixture are separated. Can you identify the extraction method used in the photograph on the right?

Answer
Flotation.

Chemistry in Action

Extracting gold

Gold is not an abundant metal. It usually occurs at extremely low concentrations mixed with other elements, such as oxygen or sulfur. Getting gold out of rock usually involves a chemical extraction process. Gold does not dissolve in water, but will dissolve in a solution of cyanide. Cyanides are organic acids (*see* vol. 8: pp. 38–45) that contain a nitrogen atom. Low-grade ores, which contain little gold, are broken into small chunks and are placed on lined pads in heaps. A weak solution of cyanide is poured over the heap. The cyanide trickles down through the heap, dissolving the gold as it goes. The solution containing the gold is collected from the bottom of the heap.

Higher-grade ores are processed in slightly different ways depending on what is mixed with the gold. The ore is first ground into a powder. Ores containing sulfur and carbon are roasted at high temperatures to turn the gold into an oxide ore. Sulfide ores that have no carbon are heated to lower temperatures to remove the sulfide and turn the ore into an oxide. Ores that are already oxides are simply crushed. The high-grade oxide ores are then treated with cyanide to dissolve the gold. The slurry is passed over activated carbon (carbon that

has been heat treated to give it a large surface area). The gold sticks to the carbon and the slurry is drained off.

The carbon is washed with another solution of cyanide to redissolve the gold. The carbon can then be recycled. The gold is removed from the solution by electrolysis or by chemical substitution with another element. The gold is melted into bars that contain 90 percent gold and then sent to a refinery where the gold is turned into 99.99 percent pure bars.

▲ *Miners panning for gold use gravity to separate gold nuggets from other bits of stone and sediment. Gold is heavy and remains at the bottom of the pan when it is swirled in the water.*

to mining, they are usually restricted to metals such as iron, copper, zinc, gold, silver, tin, platinum, aluminum, titanium, and magnesium. These metals are used

in making products that people use every day.

Metals are used in many different applications because of their properties

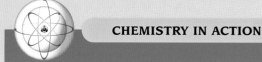

(*see* vol. 6). Metals are ductile, malleable, conductive, and lustrous. Each of these properties make metal ideal for a wide variety of applications.

Ductility and malleability are two related properties of metals. Ductility refers to the ability to draw a metal into a wire. Copper is one of the most common metals used in wire but other metals are also used for their ductility. Iron is drawn into wire and used to make chain link and other fence material. Malleability is the ability to pound metal into different shapes. Gold is one of the most malleable metals. A single gram of gold (0.035 ounces) can be pounded into a sheet that covers 1 square meter (about 10 square feet).

Metals conduct (carry) electricity. However, the conductive properties of metals are not restricted to electricity. Metals also conduct heat. The conductive ability of metals has to do with the arrangement of atoms in the metal. The atoms are tightly packed together. This

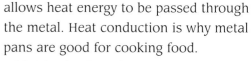

▼ *Welding is a method of joining two pieces of the same or different metals by heating.*

allows heat energy to be passed through the metal. Heat conduction is why metal pans are good for cooking food.

Metals also have luster. Lustrous objects reflect light. You have probably seen gold or silver jewelry that seems to sparkle when light shines on it. The luster of metals is also used to make mirrors. A thin coating of metal on one side of a piece of glass gives mirrors their reflective properties.

Metals can also be cast or machined into many different shapes. Metals are used to support buildings. Metal girders are shaped to withstand tremendous weight and are then bolted together. Metal can also be welded. Welding is used to join metal objects together with a bead of molten metal. A weld can be very strong.

◄ Pure gold is relatively soft and can easily be shaped into objects. This mask was made by an early South American metalworker, who used gold to make decorative and precious items.

Metals are used to make all manner of cans, jars, pans, cars, planes, and jewelry. Metal is used in a staggering array of objects. If you look around, you will see many objects that are made of metals. Metals, like plastics, are very much a part of everyday life and they have been for a very long time.

HISTORY OF METAL USE

Humans have been using metals for more than 8,000 years. The first metal known and used was gold. This is not surprising because gold is sometimes found in an elemental (uncombined) state. Gold is easily worked and does not oxidize (form a compound with oxygen) or tarnish like other metals. Gold was used mainly for jewelry and precious objects. Because gold is so malleable, it was used for decorative items rather than everyday objects.

Copper was the next metal discovered. Its use also dates back more than 8,000 years. Copper is still easy to work but is harder than gold. Copper was used to make tools and weapons. Copper can sometimes be found in its elemental state in nature but it is usually found in the minerals cuprite, malachite, azurite, chalcopyrite, and bornite. Copper had to be smelted to obtain pure copper.

The other metals that have been long known are silver, lead, tin, iron, and

Chemistry in Action

Mercury—the liquid metal

When you think of metal, you think of a hard substance. That is not true of all metals—mercury is the only metal that is a liquid at room temperature. The common name for mercury is quicksilver. Mercury has a high density, more than 13 times that of water. Mercury is used in many different products. It is found in some thermometers, fluorescent and mercury-vapor lights, and dental fillings. Its use is being phased out because it is poisonous and can damage the environment.

Chemistry in Action

Cast iron

You have probably seen black cast iron skillets (below). They have been used for cooking since the early 1700s. Cast iron is also used in other products such as car engines, pipes, and tools. Cast iron has small amounts of carbon and silicon added to give it stronger properties. Cast iron is melted in a furnace and then poured into a mold. This process is quick and relatively inexpensive and is used to produce large quantities of cast iron products.

These first seven metals were widely used but only a few new metals were discovered. Before 1800, the only metals in frequent use were gold, silver, copper, lead, mercury, iron, tin, platinum, antimony, bismuth, zinc, and arsenic. In the 1800s, many new metals were discovered. One of these metals, aluminum, was first produced in 1825. For a time, it was one of the most precious metals because scientists could not figure out a way to make elemental aluminum. In fact, aluminum was priced higher than gold and platinum. It was not until 1854 that a commercial process was found and the price of aluminum fell by 90 percent over the next 10 years.

In 1885 the process for producing aluminum was improved and the annual production of aluminum was 15 metric tons. The Hall–Héroult process was discovered in 1886 and production increased. By 1900 the annual.

mercury. Each of these metals was discovered more than 3,000 years ago. None of these metals occurs in its elemental state in nature so they must be processed either by smelting or at least some type of heating. Tin was one of the important finds because, if mixed with copper, it forms an alloy called bronze. Bronze is much stronger than either copper or tin. This alloy allowed for much harder tools and weapons. Bronze was so important that a developmental period called the Bronze Age was named for the rise of bronze tools and weapons.

▷ Silver is another metal that has long been prized for its ornamental value. Like gold it is easy to work and can be given a high polish. However, over time silver begins to tarnish unless it is regularly cleaned to remove the layer of silver oxide that forms on the surface.

production of aluminum was 8,800 tons (8,000 metric tons). By 2005, the production of aluminum reached 26.5 million tons (24 million metric tons).

SMELTING AND ELECTROLYSIS

Smelting is the chemical reduction of an ore to extract a metal. Smelting is used to produce iron, copper, aluminum, and many other metals. Smelting uses a reducing agent such as coke or charcoal to provide electrons (negatively charged atomic particles). Coke is a carbon residue derived from coal. During smelting, high temperatures and the reducing agent change the oxidation state of the metal by removing oxygen and other elements from the ore.

The reduced metal from the ore ends up in its metallic state. The molten metal must then be separated from the slag, the by-products from the ore. Typically, the molten metal is poured off into

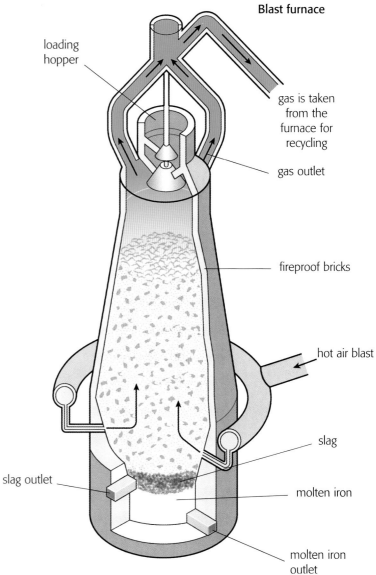

Blast furnace

loading hopper

gas is taken from the furnace for recycling

gas outlet

fireproof bricks

hot air blast

slag

molten iron

slag outlet

molten iron outlet

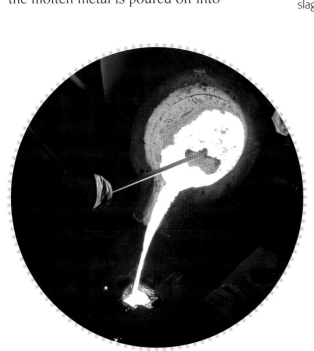

▲ Iron is separated from its ore in a blast furnace. The ore is heated to a very high temperature with a source of carbon, such as coke. Burning the coke provides heat to the furnace and also produces carbon monoxide gas. The gas oxidizes to carbon dioxide and at the same time reduces the iron ore to metallic iron. This type of reaction, where electrons are lost by the element being oxidized and gained by the element being reduced, is called a redox (reduction–oxidation) reaction (see vol. 3: pp. 26–29). The waste products, called slag, form a crust on top of the liquid metal. ◀ The metal can then be drawn out from the bottom of the furnace and poured into molds.

TRY THIS

Rusting nails

Iron objects rust when exposed to oxygen. Rust is actually an iron oxide that forms on the surface of iron objects when exposed to air. In this activity, you will explore how sealing the nail against oxygen prevents rust from forming.

Materials: two new bright nails, one galvanized nail, 3 glasses, water, vegetable oil

1. Place a nail in each glass. You may need to polish the bright nails with sandpaper. Do not polish the galvanized nail.

2. Pour water into one of the glasses with a bright nail and the glass with the galvanized nail. Dip the last nail in a little vegetable oil

▼ *From left to right the photographs show a galvanized nail, an ungalvanized nail, and an ungalvanized nail coated with oil and covered with water. Only the middle nail has rusted.*

and pour water over it. Add enough vegetable oil to completely cover the surface of the glass.

3. Leave the glasses undisturbed for several days and then observe.

The galvanized nail has not rusted because it is protected with a rust-resistant coating. The nail covered with oil has not rusted because the oil provides a protective coating, preventing oxygen getting to the nail.

molds to make ingots. The ingots may then undergo further refining to improve the purity of the metal, or they can be mixed with other metals to change the properties of the metal.

The other method of producing metals is electrolysis. Electrolysis involves passing electricity through a molten metal. In an industrial setting, electrolysis is used to manufacture sodium, aluminum, potassium, and lithium. There are two general laws that relate to electrolysis.

The first law of electrolysis states that the quantity of elements separated by passing an electrical current through a molten or dissolved salt is proportional

to the quantity of electric charge passed through the circuit.

The second law of electrolysis states that the mass of the resulting separated elements is directly proportional to the atomic masses of the elements.

These two laws set the limits for the industrial use of electrolysis. Aluminum is produced using electrolysis. The amount of energy needed to produce aluminum is huge. Aluminum processing plants are therefore sited close to sources of cheap electricity. It is common for aluminum processing to take place near hydroelectric dams because the energy is obtained cheaply.

One big advantage of electrolysis is that the by-products often have commercial value, too. For example, the electrolysis of sodium chloride to produce sodium metal also produces hydrogen and chlorine as by-products. Both of these by-products have great commercial value.

IMPROVING THE QUALITY OF METALS

One problem with many metals is that they corrode, or oxidize, easily. Rust is a good example of corrosion. Rust forms on iron when iron is exposed to oxygen. The rust that forms is iron oxide. This compound can weaken the metal. One way to protect metal is to treat the surface to prevent corrosion.

Iron is widely used but suffers from corrosion. One way to protect iron is to galvanize it. In the galvanization process, a thin layer of zinc is plated onto the surface of an iron object. The zinc on the surface oxidizes to a hard layer of zinc oxide and protects the iron below. As long as the zinc oxide layer is intact, no oxygen reaches the iron below.

Galvanizing is not the only method for protecting the surface of a metal. Painting is a common method of protecting metal. Paint seals off the metal's surface from oxygen. Paint has a drawback in that it can peel or be easily scratched, exposing the metal underneath. A more durable coating is electroplating. Electroplating is the deposition of a different metal onto the surface of another metal through an electrochemical process. The metals chosen for plating have to be carefully selected because the most durable finishes have a more active metal plated onto a less active metal. You can learn more about the activity of metals and electroplating in Volume 6 (pp. 12–13).

Another method for protecting metal surfaces is anodizing. Anodizing is often used to protect aluminum but it can be used on titanium, too. Anodizing places a layer of aluminum oxide onto the

This iron fence has been coated with a layer of zinc in a process called galvanization. Galvanizing iron prevents it from rusting by protecting it from the air.

surface of aluminum. This is achieved by placing the cleaned aluminum object into a sulfuric acid bath. Then, an electric current is passed through the aluminum. As the term *anodizing* implies, the aluminum object is connected to the anode (positive electrode). The reaction between the metal and the acid causes a hard, noncorroding layer of aluminum oxide to form on the surface. The oxidized surface is porous enough that dye can be added, giving the aluminum a colored protective surface.

ALLOYS

As you have learned, metals have many different properties that make them ideal for certain applications. It has also been

Key Terms

- **Corrosion:** The slow wearing away of metals by chemical attack.
- **Crystal lattice:** The arrangement of atoms in a solid.
- **Oxidation:** The addition of oxygen to a compound.
- **Solution:** A mixture of two or more elements or compounds in a single phase (solid, liquid, or gas).

mentioned that some metals can be mixed together to give even better properties. For example, copper is one of the earliest metals used by people. Copper is soft enough to work but hard

◁ *Stainless steel is an alloy used for many household items, such as sinks and faucets. These items would rust rapidly if they were made of ordinary steel.*

Aluminum alloys are used to make the bodies for subway trains. Such alloys are light but strong and can be molded into different shapes.

enough to make tools and weapons. When tin is added to copper, it makes bronze. Bronze was very useful because it still had a relatively low melting point and it could easily be worked. However, it was much harder than pure copper. As a result, bronze tools and weapons were much stronger.

When metals are mixed together, the result is called an alloy. Bronze is not the only metal alloy. In fact, very few metals in use are pure metals. Alloys have better properties and they are often cheap to produce. Alloys are actually a special type of solution (*see* vol. 5: p. 42).

One common alloy is steel. Steel is an alloy of iron and carbon. The carbon helps strengthen the steel. Carbon hardens steel by preventing iron atoms in their crystal lattice structure from sliding past each other. Iron forms many alloys and they all have different properties. Another iron alloy is stainless steel. Stainless steel contains iron, carbon,

and at least 10 percent chromium. Stainless steel is naturally resistant to oxidation and maintains a shiny surface.

Aluminum is a commonly used metal. However, aluminum is almost never used as a pure metal. Aluminum alloys are widely used. Aluminum is often alloyed with copper, manganese, magnesium, or silicon. The different aluminum alloys all have different properties. Aluminum is used for making cans, airplanes, cars, kitchen utensils, wire, roofing, and tools. The uses of aluminum are almost endless. When designing a mechanical or structural part, an engineer can select the required properties and specify a particular alloy to be used. Aluminum alloys are useful because they are not only strong and resistant to corrosion, but they are also very light. As has already been noted, aluminum and its alloys can be anodized to make them brightly colored and even more corrosion resistant.

See Also ...
*The Metals,
Vol. 5: pp. 34–43.
Metals and
Metalloids,
Vol. 6: pp. 1–65.*

3 Chemistry and the Environment

Water, air, and land are the liquid, gas, and solid that make up the surface of the planet on which we live.

One of the major factors in shaping our environment is chemical reactions. The solids, liquids, and gases that make up our planet react with each other to form new substances. These in turn may take part in further chemical reactions.

The Earth is made up of three important substances—air, land, and water. Chemicals in air, land, and water are constantly reacting and interacting with each other.

Air makes up the atmosphere of our planet. Air consists of a number of different gaseous elements and compounds (*see* vol. 1: pp. 16–23). Land is the solid surface of Earth. Land is made up mostly of rocks, which contain many different chemical elements in a solid form. Water is found in oceans, lakes, and rivers. It is also found as a gas in the atmosphere. It can also be chemically bound into different rocks. Water itself is a chemical compound of hydrogen and oxygen. Water is also a solvent (*see* vol. 4: pp. 34–45) that dissolves many different compounds.

EARTH'S ATMOSPHERE

Earth's atmosphere is a mixture of gases. Nitrogen makes up about 78 percent of the atmosphere, and oxygen makes up about 21 percent.

▶ Plants and some single-celled organisms use sunlight to make sugars out of carbon dioxide and water—a process called photosynthesis. The oxygen in the atmosphere is a by-product of this process.

The remaining 1 percent is made up of many different gases.

Earth's atmosphere has been evolving since the planet first formed more than 4.5 billion years ago. At first, the atmosphere was probably mostly hydrogen and helium. As the Earth cooled about 3.5 billion years ago, the atmosphere transformed into one of water vapor (H_2O), carbon dioxide (CO_2), and ammonia (NH_3) with no oxygen. About 3.3 billion years ago, the first organisms started to add oxygen to the atmosphere as a by-product of

◀ These pie charts show the proportions of gases in Earth's atmosphere. Almost 99 percent of the atmosphere is made of nitrogen and oxygen.

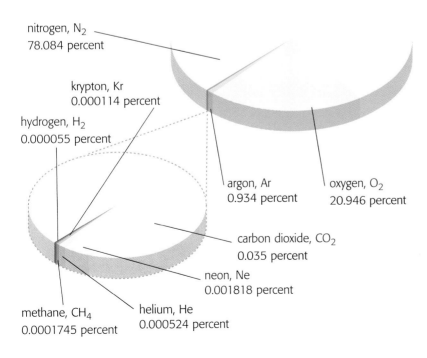

nitrogen, N_2
78.084 percent

krypton, Kr
0.000114 percent

hydrogen, H_2
0.000055 percent

argon, Ar
0.934 percent

oxygen, O_2
20.946 percent

carbon dioxide, CO_2
0.035 percent

neon, Ne
0.001818 percent

methane, CH_4
0.0001745 percent

helium, He
0.000524 percent

photosynthesis. In photosynthesis, plants and some single-celled organisms use energy from sunlight to make sugars from carbon dioxide and water.

THE ATMOSPHERE AND OXIDATION

Earth's atmosphere surrounds the planet and takes part in the chemistry of the environment. Burning and rusting are a result of two chemical reactions involving oxygen from the atmosphere. Originally, any reaction involving oxygen was called an oxidation reaction. Now the meaning of oxidation has been extended to include any reaction in which electrons are lost. This definition covers the original meaning. Burning is a kind of oxidation reaction called combustion where oxygen reacts rapidly with something else, producing heat and light. Rusting is an oxidation reaction where oxygen reacts with iron.

Animals use oxygen in various biochemical reactions in the body. These oxidation reactions are used to release energy from food.

▼ *Smog over Los Angeles, California, is caused by pollution from automobiles reacting with sunlight. Although Los Angeles still suffers from smog, cleaner automobile emissions have improved the air quality.*

TRY THIS

Rusting

Rusting is an oxidation reaction in which iron reacts with oxygen to produce iron oxide, or rust.

Materials: steel wool pad, plastic cup, and water

1. If the steel wool pad has soap in it, wash it thoroughly to remove all soap.

2. Place the steel wool in the plastic cup and add some water to the cup, but make sure the steel wool is above the top of the water.

3. Leave the cup undisturbed overnight and then observe how it looks the next day.

You should see that the steel wool has turned reddish from the rust. Where do you think the oxygen for this reaction came from?

Answer
The oxygen came from the air.

AIR POLLUTION

When humans began burning large quantities of coal and oil, the atmosphere began to suffer. The smoke from burning wood or fossil fuels is visible pollution. The more fuel is burned, the more the smoke becomes a problem. The smoke and other chemicals in it can cause smog—a mixture of smoke and fog. In the United States, thanks to efforts to reduce air pollution, smog is now only seen over some of the larger cities. However, visible smog is only one type of air pollution.

Some of the products from burning fossil fuels are not easy to see but can cause problems too. These pollutants include carbon dioxide, carbon monoxide, sulfur oxides, nitrogen oxides, and lead. Fossil fuels are made of hydrocarbons—chemical combinations of hydrogen and carbon. The complete combustion of a hydrocarbon yields carbon dioxide and water as products. However, complete combustion is not always possible when fossil fuels are burned. As a result, both

A Closer LOOK

Carbon dioxide in the atmosphere

One concern about the atmosphere is the increasing level of carbon dioxide–a greenhouse gas. When fossil fuels are burned, carbon dioxide is released. Have you ever wondered how much carbon dioxide is released when gasoline is burned?

One gallon of gasoline (3.8 liters) weighs 6.3 pounds (2.9 kg). Because gasoline is about 87 percent carbon, the carbon in a gallon of gasoline weighs 5.5 pounds (6.3 lbs x 0.87). During combustion, each carbon atom joins with two oxygen atoms from the atmosphere to form carbon dioxide. But two oxygen atoms are $2\frac{2}{3}$ times heavier than a single carbon atom. Therefore, the mass of the oxygen that joins with the carbon is 14.7 pounds (5.5 lbs x $2\frac{2}{3}$). The total mass of the carbon dioxide is the mass of the carbon plus the mass of the oxygen, which makes a total of about 20 pounds of carbon dioxide!

Key Terms

- **Combustion:** A chemical reaction in which oxygen reacts rapidly with something else, producing heat and light.
- **Greenhouse gases:** Gases such as carbon dioxide and methane that trap heat in Earth's atmosphere.
- **Hydrocarbon:** Chemical made from hydrogen and carbon atoms.
- **Photosynthesis:** Process by which plants use sunlight to turn carbon dioxide and water into sugars.

carbon dioxide and carbon monoxide are produced. Inhaling high levels of carbon monoxide can cause headaches, fatigue, respiratory problems, and, in extreme cases, death.

Carbon dioxide is a particular problem because it is also a greenhouse gas.

Certain gases, such as carbon dioxide, water vapor, and methane, trap heat in the atmosphere. The energy received from the Sun in the form of visible light is absorbed by Earth's surface, which re-radiates it at infrared wavelengths. Some of this infrared energy is trapped by these greenhouse gases. Without some carbon dioxide in the atmosphere to trap infrared, Earth would be much colder. As fossil fuels are burned, however, the heat-trapping ability of the atmosphere increases, resulting in global warming.

Nitrogen and sulfur also bond with oxygen during combustion, forming nitrogen oxide and sulfur oxides. Some of these oxides react with water in the atmosphere to create acid rain. The problems surrounding acid rain will be covered later in this chapter.

Another air pollution problem comes from lead added to gasoline. When gasoline is burned, lead is also released into the atmosphere. Lead damages many human organs and causes damage to the nervous system. Between 1970

Chemistry in Action

Chemistry and life

One easy test used to identify minerals is based on their hardness. Geologists use the Mohs' hardness scale to rank minerals. This table shows the minerals that are ranked 1 through 10; with 1 being the softest. A harder mineral will scratch any softer mineral. For example, quartz can scratch a knife blade and a knife blade can scratch calcite, but only a diamond can scratch a diamond.

Mineral	Hardness
Diamond	10
Corundum	9
Topaz	8
Quartz	7
(steel file)	6.5
Orthoclase	6
(window glass or knife blade)	5.5
Apatite	5
Fluorite	4
Calcite	3
(fingernail)	2.5
Gypsum	2
Talc	1

◀ The mineral hematite is an important iron ore. It is an oxide and has the formula Fe_2O_3.

and 1997, air emissions of lead into the air in the United States were reduced from 320,000 tons to 4,000 tons (290,240 to 3,630 metric tons) per year, largely because lead was phased out of gasoline.

MINERALS

Minerals are naturally formed solids with characteristic crystal structures and specific chemical formulas. Minerals can

◀ *The stone in Red Rock Canyon State Park, California, is a type of sandstone. Sandstone is a sedimentary rock. It is made by the slow laying down of tiny grains (sediment) of eroded rocks. These layers of sediment are eventually pressed together to form solid sandstone.*

crystal shape, hardness, tendency to break in preferred directions, color, and density. It is worth noting that color, the most obvious characteristic, is often the least reliable identifier.

ROCKS

Rocks are made up of minerals that are stuck together. Rocks can be made up of many different minerals or just one mineral. The minerals in rocks tell geologists about the history of how the rocks formed.

Rocks are divided into three groups: igneous, sedimentary, and metamorphic. Igneous rocks are those that solidify from molten materials. Igneous rocks include basalt and granite. Basalt forms when lava cools quickly so the mineral crystals are very small. Granite cools very slowly so the mineral crystals are able to grow large.

Sedimentary rocks form by materials being deposited by water, ice, wind, or chemical action. The sediment deposits are then cemented or pressed together to form a solid rock. Two common examples of sedimentary rocks are limestone and sandstone. A chemical process forms limestone when calcium

be composed of simple chemical compounds, or they can be quite complex. It may seem surprising but ice is actually a mineral of water because it meets the above characteristics.

Minerals can be identified by their physical properties. These properties are influenced by the chemical composition and crystal structure of the mineral. They include the quality and intensity of light reflected from the mineral, external

▼ *Monument Rocks in Kansas are made from limestone that has been carved by wind and rain. Limestone is a sedimentary rock made mostly of calcium carbonate ($CaCO_3$).*

▲ *The layer of white rock is quartzite, which is a type of metamorphic rock made from sandstone. The surrounding black rock is gabbro, an igneous rock.*

carbonate (CaCO$_3$) precipitates (separates) out of warm seawater. Sandstone is formed when sand is deposited and is then cemented together by another mineral.

Metamorphic rocks form from either igneous, sedimentary, or even other metamorphic rocks. Metamorphic rocks are changed (metamorphosed), by high heat, high pressure, or both. Two examples of metamorphic rocks are marble and quartzite. Marble is limestone that has metamorphosed. It is harder and more crystalline than limestone. Quartzite is metamorphosed sandstone. High heat and pressure cause the quartz crystals in the sandstone to grow and fuse together.

THE ROCK CYCLE

One type of rock can be transformed into other types of rock. Heat and pressure can cause a rock to metamorphose. If there is enough heat and pressure, the rock can melt. When it cools again, it will form igneous rock. Weathering and erosion are also responsible for changing rocks.

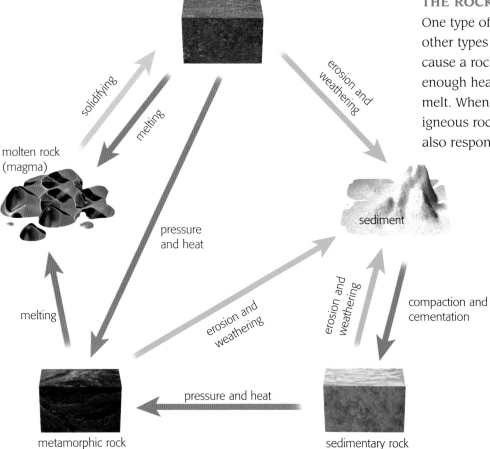

igneous rock

solidifying

melting

erosion and weathering

molten rock (magma)

pressure and heat

sediment

melting

erosion and weathering

erosion and weathering

compaction and cementation

pressure and heat

metamorphic rock

sedimentary rock

◀ *The rock cycle describes the way that one form of rock can develop into another. Igneous rock, for example, can be eroded into sediment. The sediment can then be squeezed and cemented to form sedimentary rock.*

Chemical weathering

The acids in rainwater cause the chemical weathering of limestone, which is made mostly of calcium carbonate. In the following activity, vinegar (a weak acid) is used in place of rainwater, and chalk (calcium carbonate) is used in place of limestone to simulate chemical weathering.

Materials: piece of sidewalk or blackboard chalk, vinegar, and a glass

Fill the glass about half full of vinegar. Add the chalk and observe.

The bubbles you see forming are carbon dioxide. The acid is neutralized by the calcium carbonate and produces carbon dioxide as a product.

WEATHERING AND EROSION

Weathering and erosion are processes that break rocks into smaller parts. Weathering is the process of breaking down rocks into smaller fragments. Erosion is the removal and transport of these small parts by wind, water, or ice. Weathering may be mechanical or chemical. Mechanical weathering is any process that breaks rocks using physical force. Such physical force may result from ice, water, wind, gravity, tree roots, or the action of animals.

Chemical weathering is the chemical breakdown of rocks and minerals. Water is the most obvious source of chemical weathering. Carbon dioxide is easily dissolved in water. When this happens, it forms carbonic acid. This is a reaction that can move in both directions—the

▷ *Frost action has split this rock in Arizona. Water in gaps in the rock froze and expanded, exerting forces on the rock that have caused it to split.*

◀ *These spectacular cave formations were created by the erosion of limestone by rainwater. As water seeps through the ground above the cave, acids in the water erode some of the calcium carbonate in the limestone. As the water drips from the roof of the cave, small amounts of calcium carbonate are left behind. The gradual buildup of calcium carbonate forms the stalactites that hang from the cave's ceiling and the stalagmites that grow up from the floor of the cave.*

▲ *Acid rain has caused these stone sculptures to erode. Acid rain is a result of pollution caused by burning fossil fuels.*

carbonic acid can turn back into carbon dioxide and water. Eventually, the reaction reaches equilibrium so that as much carbonic acid is made as is broken down. This reaction looks like this:

$$CO_2 + H_2O \leftrightarrow H_2CO_3$$

This weak acid will react with many minerals and eventually break them down.

Rainwater is naturally acidic, but nitrogen oxides and sulfur oxides from the burning of fossil fuels react with rainwater to form nitric acid and sulfuric acid, making rainwater even more acidic. This extra acidity greatly increases the rate of chemical weathering caused by water. Acid rain affects objects made of limestone, marble, or granite. It also affects metals such as bronze.

Acidic rainwater affects objects on the surface and also below ground. In areas with limestone, water can carve through the rock and enlarge fractures to form

TRY THIS

Hard water, soft water

Materials: rainwater or distilled water, tap water, 3 small glasses, marker, Epsom salts, and dishwashing soap

Both rainwater and distilled water are much like what people call "soft water." These liquids contain few ions, atoms that have gained or lost electrons. Epsom salt is magnesium sulfate ($MgSO_4$). When it dissolves in water, it is like "hard water."

1. Fill two glasses about half full of rainwater or distilled water. Fill the third glass about half full of tap water.

2. Add about 1 spoonful of Epsom salts to one of the glasses containing rainwater or distilled water.

3. Add three drops of dishwashing soap to each glass.

4. Stir the water in each glass rapidly. Observe the results.

The glass with only distilled water or rainwater should be quite foamy and the glass containing magnesium sulfate should have little foam. How does your tap water compare?

▲ *The glass on the left contains distilled water, which is soft. Notice the bubbles on the surface. The middle glass contains distilled water with Epsom salts added, making the water hard. Thus, the dishwashing soap does not bubble. The glass on the right is tap water. There are some bubbles on the surface but not many, so the water must be a little hard.*

caves. In the process, calcium carbonate from the limestone becomes dissolved in the water. Cave formations such as stalactites and stalagmites are made of calcium carbonate that has precipitated (separated) out from the water as it drips from the ceiling of the cave.

CHEMISTRY AND WATER

Water is a very powerful agent in erosion and weathering. Water covers about 75 percent of the Earth's surface. Most water is found in the oceans. Seawater is salty from salts that have dissolved out of rocks. The salinity (total amount

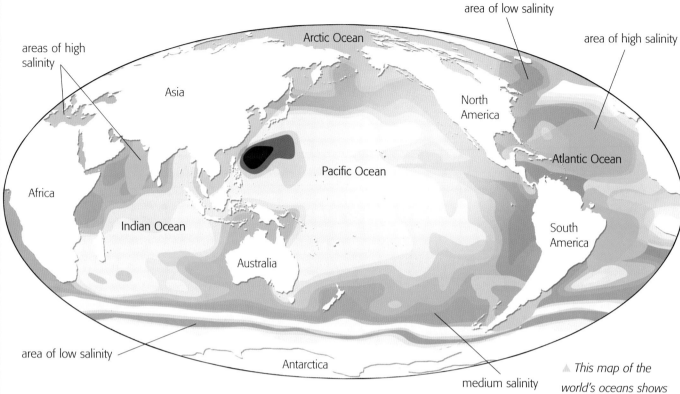

area of low salinity

area of high salinity

areas of high salinity

Arctic Ocean

Asia

North America

Atlantic Ocean

Pacific Ocean

Africa

Indian Ocean

South America

Australia

area of low salinity

Antarctica

medium salinity

▲ *This map of the world's oceans shows the salinity (salt content) of the water. Areas of low salinity are shown in purple (about 34 parts per thousand). Medium salinity is shown in blue-green (about 35 parts per thousand). High salinity is shown in bright green (about 36 parts per thousand). The salt in the world's oceans has been dissolved out of rocks.*

TRY THIS

Water cycle in a bottle

Materials: 2-liter plastic bottle with cap, ice, sand, knife

1. With the help of an adult, carefully cut the bottom off the bottle. Leave the cap on the bottle.

2. Turn the top of the bottle upside-down and add sand until the bottle is about ¼ full. Add a little water to the sand. Support the top of the bottle in loose soil or sand and place in the sun.

3. Slide the empty bottle bottom into the open end of the bottle top. Fill the bottle bottom with crushed ice.

You should notice that water droplets form on the bottle bottom. The sunlight has caused the water to evaporate from the sand, but the ice has cooled the water and caused it to condense on the bottom of the bottle.

of salt) in seawater is about 35 parts per thousand, or about 35 grams in 1 liter.

Water exists on Earth in all three phases—solid, liquid, and gas (*see* vol. 2). Water has several unusual properties. It is one of the few substances in which the solid phase will float in the liquid phase. Water also has a high boiling point and its heat capacity (the amount of heat required to raise its temperature) is also high. These properties are very important to the environment.

The oceans are an important reservoir for water on the planet, but they are not the only place water is found. Water exists as a gas in the atmosphere, as a solid at the poles and on mountaintops, and as a liquid in rain, rivers, and lakes.

Water moves through the environment in the water cycle. Energy from the sun causes water to evaporate (change from a liquid state to a gaseous state). Water vapor in the atmosphere is invisible. However, as the atmosphere cools, water

condenses into tiny droplets that you see as clouds. Some clouds hold so much water vapor that the water droplets become large enough to fall as rain. This rain runs into rivers and streams and returns to the ocean. This is the simplified version of the water cycle.

THE UNIVERSAL SOLVENT
Water dissolves many different substances and is therefore often called the universal solvent. This property of water is a result of its molecular structure. The electrons in a water molecule are not evenly distributed, so water has a slightly positive end at the oxygen atom and two slightly negative ends on the hydrogen atoms. This makes

▼ Limescale (calcium carbonate) on this washing machine element has been deposited by minerals in water. The water used in this washing machine must therefore have been hard water.

Key Terms

- **Acid rain:** Rain that has an unusually high level of acidity resulting from pollution. Acid rain causes damage to forests, lakes, and rivers.
- **Erosion:** The removal and transport of small pieces of rock by wind, water, or ice.
- **Weathering:** The processes that break rocks into smaller parts. Weathering may be mechanical, resulting from physical forces such as abrasion by ice and wind, or chemical, such as the dissolving of chemicals in rocks by water.

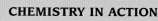

water a polar solvent (*see* vol. 1: pp. 42–55). Water dissolves many polar substances, such as salts, but does not dissolve nonpolar substances, such as oil.

You have probably heard the terms *hard water* and *soft water*. These terms are used to describe the water in your home. If you wash your hands with hard water, you may have noticed that the soap does not lather well. In soft water, the soap really lathers up but does not wash off easily. Hard water has many dissolved ions in it—atoms that have lost or gained electrons. Soap is made up of positive potassium ions and negative palmitate ions. Hard water already contains many ions so the soap does not ionize as much and does not lather well.

You may be confused by the fact that water does not dissolve oils. If you have ever had oil on your hands, you know that you can wash it off with soap. The key is

the soap. Soap changes the interaction between oil and water to enable rinsing.

The terms *soap* and *detergent* are often used to mean the same thing. However, these two terms actually describe different things. Soaps have water-soluble sodium or potassium salts attached to chemicals called fatty acids, which are made of carbon, hydrogen, and oxygen. Soaps are formed by the reaction of a strong base (*see* vol. 3: pp. 26–27) with fatty acids. Detergents are compounds that contain surfactants to dissolve oils, and they may contain abrasives for scouring. They may also contain oxidants (a substance that brings about oxidation) for bleaching, and enzymes (substances that speed up chemical reactions) to assist in breaking down organic stains. Detergents were developed because they have better cleaning properties in hard water.

▲ *The green organisms on the surface of this watercourse are algae that have grown as a result of fertilizer runoff from agriculture. Growths such as these are called algal blooms.*

See Also ...

• **What Is Matter?** Vol. 1: pp. 4–15.
• **Introducing Elements,** Vol. 1: pp. 16–23.

WATER POLLUTION

When detergents were first introduced, they contained phosphates—salts containing phosphorus. The phosphates were released in the wastewater and found their way into rivers and lakes. Phosphorus is an important plant nutrient. Water plants and algae quickly used this extra phosphorus. The rapid growth of these plants killed off fish and other animals living in the water. In the 1970s, phosphates were replaced in detergents, and the problem has lessened.

Phosphorus is not the only pollutant found in water. Other common pollutants include pesticides, fertilizers, petroleum, acids, bases, and heavy metals. Each of these pollutants can affect organisms living in an aquatic ecosystem. Once water is polluted, it is often difficult and very expensive to clean up.

DRINKING WATER

Drinking water comes from two main sources: surface water and groundwater. Surface water includes rivers and lakes. Surface water is often exposed to many different pollutants, and these must be removed before they enter the water system. Groundwater is water found underground in geologic structures. Groundwater is sometimes filtered as it passes through the ground into the groundwater supply, or aquifer. While filtering removes some impurities from the water, it may not remove all of them. Also, if groundwater becomes polluted, it is very difficult, if not impossible, to clean it up.

Humans need clean drinking water. Because there are so many different pollutants, water must be treated to remove the pollutants. Water may be filtered through sand and activated charcoal (charcoal with a very high surface area). These remove various impurities. The water may also be exposed to ultraviolet radiation or ozone to kill microorganisms. Other treatments may be needed to remove heavy metals from the water. The final step before adding the water to the supply system is adding chlorine to kill any remaining microorganisms from the treatment and to keep the water from being contaminated by other microorganisms while in the pipes.

▼ This filtration bed forms part of a water treatment plant. To make water safe for drinking, several processes are necessary. One of the most important of these is filtration, in which water is cleaned by passing it through sand.

4 Chemistry in Medicine

When you are sick, a physician might give you medicine to get you well again. That medicine will contain chemicals that have been tried and tested to help your body recover. Sometimes, the chemicals are based on natural remedies that are hundreds or thousands of years old.

In the past, it was not as easy to get medical care as it is today. Then, if you got sick or were injured, it was much more likely that you would die from an infection or even from the "remedy"!

Throughout history, people have relied on various natural remedies to treat illness and injury. Often the remedies came from parts of plants. Sometimes they worked well, but not always.

In ancient Greece, the physician Hippocrates (460–377 B.C.E.) gave patients a bitter powder derived from the bark of willow trees to help cure headaches, muscle aches, general pains, and fevers. The Egyptians, Sumerians, and Assyrians had used this knowledge even before Hippocrates.

When scientists began to look at natural remedies such as willow bark, they found that some had a basis in science. Italian, French, and German pharmacists isolated the active ingredient in willow bark between

◢ Salicylic acid occurs in the bark of willow trees. The chemical has been used to treat pains and fevers since ancient times.

1826 and 1829. The ingredient was called salicylic acid ($C_7H_6O_3$), and later it was treated to make it less acidic. It was then marketed as aspirin, which is still available.

NATURAL SOURCES

Many modern medicines have been developed from herbal remedies. Opium, which comes from the seedpods of poppy plants, has been used for centuries as a painkiller. Opium contains a number of medically useful chemicals, including morphine and codeine. Using morphine as a base, modern chemists developed a wide range of drugs that include heroin,

◢ The Greek physician Hippocrates wrote about the healing properties of willow bark in the 5th century B.C.E. However, he did not know why it had these properties.

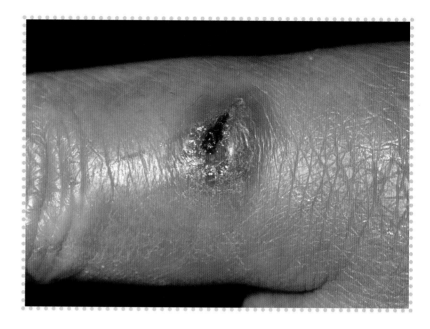

meperidine, and fentanyl. Similarly coca leaves, used by native South Americans to combat altitude sickness, are the source of the local anesthetic cocaine.

ANTISEPTICS AND SURGERY

Most surgery is much safer now than it was in times past. One of the first advancements in making it safe was the prevention of infection. Until the second half of the 19th century, it was common for surgical wounds to develop sepsis, or infections. In 1865, a Scottish doctor named Joseph Lister (1827–1912) suggested that sepsis was caused by living organisms. He used carbolic acid (C_6H_5OH), or phenol, to clean his instruments before performing surgery. Carbolic acid was the first antiseptic. Lister showed that this procedure could successfully prevent sepsis. His work was developed by other scientists to make many more antiseptics. With modern antiseptics, the risk of infections after surgery has been greatly reduced.

▲ *Antiseptics are often used to prevent cuts from becoming infected with bacteria or other microorganisms.*

Chemistry in Action

Search for new drugs

Scientists are always searching for new treatments for diseases. Sometimes, these scientists work with "medicine men" who still use their traditional medicines. They hope to develop new drugs from the natural remedies. Other scientists take samples of plants in remote parts of the world, hoping to discover new cures.

▶ *A group of scientists collects plant specimens in Guyana. The scientists hope the plants contain the chemical ingredients that can be made into cures for diseases.*

Chemistry in Action

Antimicrobial soap

If you look at the label of many household cleaning products, you will see that the label indicates that they are antimicrobial or antibacterial. *Antimicrobial* means the products contain chemical agents that kill microorganisms such as bacteria and fungi. These products are useful in the kitchen because they can kill the disease-causing organisms that could contaminate food. Scientists worry that overuse of these cleaners might allow bacteria to develop resistance to the chemicals. New chemicals would then be needed.

Anesthetics fall into three major groups: local, regional, and general. Local anesthetics prevent the transmission of nerve impulses without causing unconsciousness. Some are based on carboxylic acids, which form salts called esters (*see* vol. 8: pp. 47–48). Ester-based anesthetics, such as procaine, amethocaine, and cocaine, act very quickly, but they may cause allergic reactions. Other local anesthetics are based on amides, in which an alcohol group is replaced by a nitrogen group. The effects of amide-based anesthetics, such as lidocaine, prilocaine, bupivicaine,

ANESTHETICS

Another big advance in surgery was the development of anesthesia. An anesthetic agent blocks the perception of pain and other sensations. This allows surgery to be performed with the patient not feeling any pain. The early anesthetics included opium, marijuana, belladonna, and alcohol. These dulled the sensation of pain but did not remove it.

In 1844, a dentist at Massachusetts General Hospital named Horace Wells anesthetized a patient before removing a tooth. The anesthetic he used was nitrous oxide, or "laughing gas" (N_2O), and it worked well. Two years later, William Morton, another dentist at the same hospital, gave his patient diethyl ether ($C_4H_{10}O$) before operating. The patient reported that he had felt no pain.

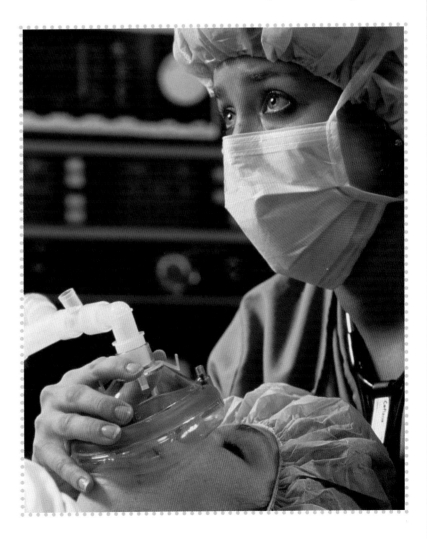

▶ *A physician administers a mixture of air and isoflurane ($C_3H_2OClF_5$) anesthetic. Some anesthetics are inhaled, as here, and some are injected intravenously (into the blood supply).*

levobupivicaine, ropivicaine, and dibucaine, last longer. A physician will select the local anesthetic appropriate for the patient's illness.

Regional anesthetics affect a large part of the body but not the brain. They are used to target specific nerves so the perception of pain is blocked for a large area such as an arm or leg.

A general anesthetic causes a state of total unconsciousness. Administering a general anesthetic requires a specially trained doctor called an anesthesiologist. Usually, when general anesthesia is used for surgery, a number of different drugs are used to produce the desired effect in the patient.

ANTIBIOTICS

Physicians often give antibiotics to people suffering as a result of bacterial infections. Antibiotics are drugs that slow the spread of bacteria or kill them without affecting the patient. Antibiotics are the largest group of antimicrobials.

Other antimicrobials are called antivirals, antifungals, and antiparasitics since they kill viruses, fungi, and other parasites.

Antibiotics work by targeting specific biochemical functions in bacteria. For example, an antibiotic might interfere with the ability of bacteria to produce proteins for their cell walls. Thus, the cell walls do not form properly, and the bacteria die rather than reproduce. Another antibiotic might target the biochemical mechanism that oxidizes glucose into energy (*see* vol. 9: p. 32). If bacteria cannot produce energy, they die.

Antibiotics are usually derived from natural sources. In 1932, a German chemist named Gerhard Domagk (1895–1964) synthesized a sulfonamide (a kind of amide) that killed bacteria. This synthetic drug was the first of a class called sulfa drugs. These seemed ideal because they could be readily synthesized in the laboratory. When World War II (1939–1945) broke out, soldiers were issued packets of sulfa

▼ Drugs are made in a variety of formats, such as tablets and capsules (below). Others are liquid, to be administered as an injection or swallowed. Yet others are gaseous, such as anesthetics and inhalants. The format helps the drug to be delivered to the right place in the body.

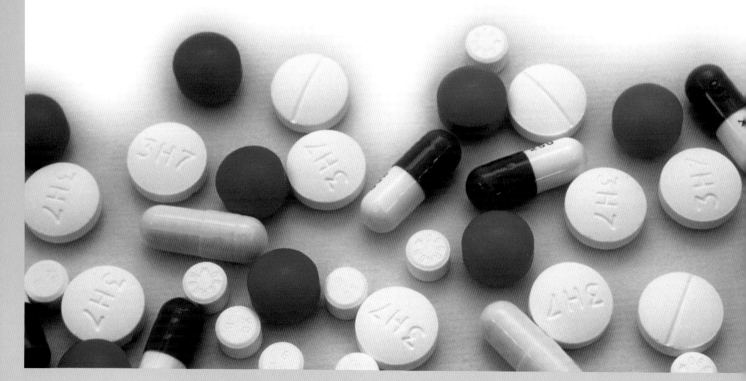

History

Alexander Fleming

Alexander Fleming (1881–1955) was a Scottish biologist and pharmacologist. Fleming is best known for his work with antibiotics. In 1922, he isolated a compound from the fungus *Penicillium notatum* that could kill bacteria. His discovery was accidental. He was studying *Staphylococcus* bacteria and one of his petri dishes became infected with *Penicillium* mold. He noticed that the mold actually killed the bacteria on the dish. His observations and work led to the first antibiotic, penicillin.

▷ *A colony of the fungus* Penicillium notatum *in a petri dish.*

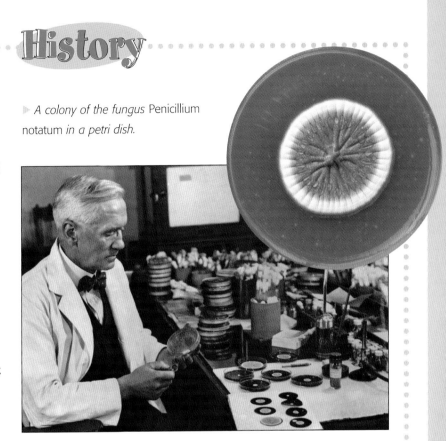

▷ *Alexander Fleming was a brilliant researcher, but he also had a reputation for untidiness. Here, he is working with bacteria cultures in St. Mary's Hospital, London, England.*

drugs to sprinkle on battlefield wounds. The drugs saved countless lives of wounded soldiers. Sulfa drugs can stop bacteria from growing, but they cannot usually kill the bacteria. These drugs were largely replaced by new and cheaper-to-produce antibiotics in the 1950s and 1960s. Sulfa drugs are still used but they are not common.

One of the problems associated with antibiotics is that bacteria can develop

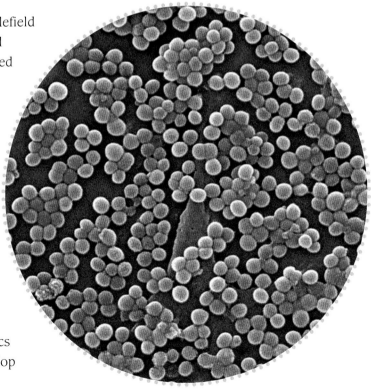

◁ *The MRSA bacterium* Staphylococcus aureus *can cause infections in surgical wounds. It is now resistant to many antibiotic drugs. This image is magnified 2,000 times.*

▲ This girl is helping to test a new drug that eases respiratory disorders. The computer screen in front of her shows the levels of oxygen and carbon dioxide in her bloodstream.

processes and try to discover how these might help produce new medicines. If a beneficial medical application for a drug is found, it may become licensed as a medicine. In the United States, the Food and Drug Administration oversees the licensing of drugs.

The medical drug industry produces huge quantities of medicines for treating conditions such as high blood pressure, diabetes, depression, anxiety, high cholesterol levels, and sleep disorders. The cost of finding new medicinal drugs is very expensive. Once the drug has been manufactured, it has to be tested to make sure that it works effectively— and that there are no bad side effects.

Developing new drugs requires a thorough understanding of how different molecules stimulate the receptors on the surface of cells to cause a reaction in the cell. Many new synthesized drugs contain chemical groups that are similar to substances found in the body, or

a resistance to them. In other words, the antibiotics are no longer effective against their intended targets. To help the situation, doctors now limit the use of some antibiotics so the bacteria have less opportunity to develop resistance. Scientists also try to develop new kinds of antibiotics, but that is slow and complex work. Some physicians fear that the antibiotics they use will be useless before long.

MODERN PHARMACOLOGY

Pharmacology is the study of the chemistry of medicinal drugs. Pharmacology links chemistry and biochemistry with the interactions of the biological processes in cells. Pharmacologists look at the interactions of different chemicals with cellular

Key Terms

- **Anesthetic:** A substance that causes lack of feeling or awareness in the body.
- **Antibiotic:** A substance that destroys or slows the growth of microorganisms, including harmful bacteria and fungi.
- **Bacteria:** A very varied group of one-celled microorganisms.
- **Sulfa drugs:** Organic compounds that are used as antibacterial agents by preventing bacteria from reproducing.
- **Viruses:** Extremely small organisms, which consist of an RNA or DNA core surrounded by a protein covering.

Chemistry in Action

Brain stimulant

Prozac is the trade name for fluoxetine hydrochloride ($C_{17}H_{18}NF_3O$). Prozac has many other trade names in other countries. Prozac is widely prescribed by physicians for treating depression, obsessive–compulsive disorder, bulimia, panic disorders, and other conditions. It was developed in the late 1980s. Prozac has been widely prescribed and very successful at treating clinical depression. Recent research suggests that fluoxetine hydrochloride may increase the rate of production of new brain cells. However, the benefits of Prozac have come at a price.

By the late 1990s, allegations were made that Prozac was linked to increased suicide rates in children and young adults. This allegation led to many lawsuits, which were unsuccessful. In 2004, traces of fluoxetine hydrochloride were found in drinking water in the United Kingdom.

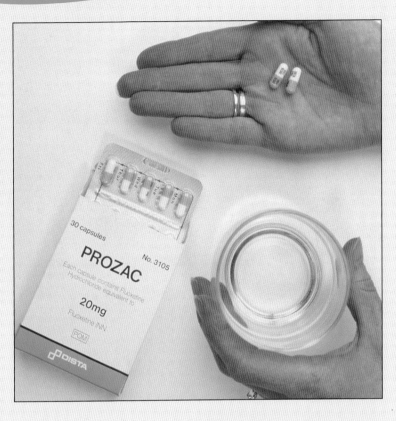

▲ Prozac is a widely prescribed antidepressant drug, but some people believe it has dangerous side effects. It is not available over the counter.

natural remedies that are already known. Pharmacologists use these known receptor sites to find molecules that will attach to them and stimulate a desired effect on one of the cell's metabolic pathways. If the tests are successful, the new drug may become a licensed medicine.

A pharmacologist has to examine some very important properties of any new drug. First, he or she looks at how the medicine is absorbed through the body's intestines, skin, or membranes. Next, the pharmacologist looks at how the drug spreads through the body. The next step is to look at how the drug is metabolized (broken down) by the body. Lastly, the pharmacologist examines how the drug is excreted from the body. This information is used to decide the best dosages to give.

Medicines are broken into two large classes. The first class is over-the-counter (OTC) medicines. These are medicines that people 18 years or older can buy from drugstores, pharmacies, gas stations, and grocery stores. Over-the-counter drugs include pain relievers, such as aspirin and ibuprofen, and medicines for coughs, colds, and fevers.

The other class of medicinal drugs is prescription-only medications (POM). The sale of these medicines is more closely controlled, and they must be prescribed by a physician and obtained from a pharmacy. POMs include many painkillers and stimulants.

METALS IN MEDICINE

Not all medicines are complex organic chemicals. Some heavy metals have also been used successfully to treat certain conditions. Before the discovery of penicillin, the sexually transmitted disease syphilis was treated either with mercury (Hg) or arsenic (As). Mercury was either given orally or rubbed into the skin to kill the syphilis bacteria. Physicians believe this treatment may

▲ *Cough medicines are commonly bought over the counter to treat minor colds that do not need prescription drugs.*

▼ *A fragment of arsenic ore. Arsenic was once used as a cure for syphilis.*

have killed the syphilis, but unfortunately large numbers of patients ended up with mercury poisoning. The use of mercury continued until the mid-19th century.

Until the 1930s, arsenic was also used as a treatment for syphilis. Then, it was replaced by sulfa drugs. Arsenic provided patients with a short-term "cure" for the symptoms of syphilis, but the disease often returned. There was also a high rate of death among patients either from chronic (long-term) or acute (short-term) arsenic poisoning. Physicians had more success when treating syphilis using a combination of arsenic, mercury, and bismuth (Bi).

These treatments seem primitive, but heavy metals are still used in medicine. Gold (Au) is still used as a

Chemistry in Action

Heavy metal poisoning

Sometimes, there are large concentrations of heavy metals such as mercury (Hg), lead (Pb), and cadmium (Cd) in the environment. These can accumulate to dangerous levels within the body and produce a condition called heavy metal poisoning. Symptoms vary with the particular heavy metal and with the amount in the body but may include vomiting, headaches, and sweating. Treatment for heavy metal poisoning is usually a chelation therapy. A chelating agent is given to the patient, and the heavy metal is attracted to the agent. The heavy metal bonds tightly to the agent and is then filtered out of the blood. This treatment is long and painful and is not always successful.

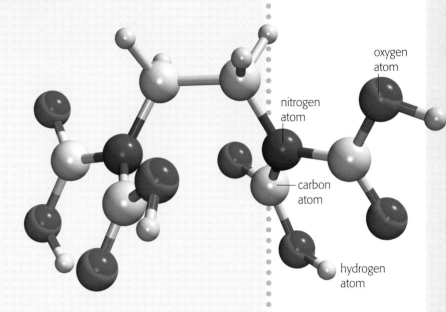

oxygen atom

nitrogen atom

carbon atom

hydrogen atom

▲ *EDTA is a chelating agent that is sometimes used in root-canal dentistry. It has the chemical formula* $C_{10}H_{16}N_2O_8$.

treatment for rheumatoid arthritis, a disease that causes the immune system to attack the body's joints. Gold salts are injected into the body in small doses every week. The effects of the treatment are not seen for between four and six months or until $\frac{1}{20}$ ounce (1 g) of gold has been injected. This treatment must be continued indefinitely to remain effective.

Radioactive metals are also used in medicine. One such example is the use of mildly radioactive iodine (I) to treat problems with the thyroid gland. The patient drinks the radioactive iodine, which concentrates in the thyroid.

The radiation destroys noncancerous nodules. This treatment is very effective for treating an overactive thyroid. The advantage of this treatment is that in only a few days the radioactive iodine passes out of the patient's system.

CHEMOTHERAPY

Chemotherapy is a method of cancer treatment. Cancer is a disease in which uncontrolled cell division results in the invasion and destruction of healthy tissues by unhealthy cells. The aim of chemotherapy is to target the cancerous cells and destroy them without harming the surrounding healthy cells.

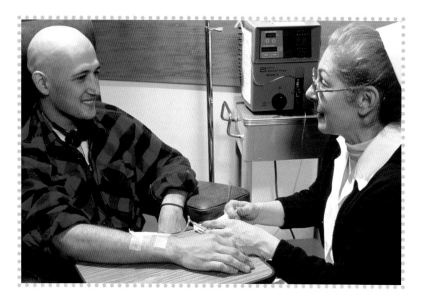

A physician gives a patient an injection of cancer-fighting drugs.

chemotherapy drugs are based on substances extracted from plants or animals. For example, mitomycin C contains products from a bacterium called *Streptomyces lavendulae*.

The dose of a chemotherapy drug must be large enough to affect the rapidly growing cancer cells, but it must not be toxic to the patient. Physicians carefully monitor the dosage and its effects on the patient, some of which may be very unpleasant. Some side effects are specific to a particular drug, and others are common to most of the chemotherapy drugs. Common side effects suffered by patients during chemotherapy include hair loss, feeling sick and vomiting, anemia (reduction in red blood cells), and damage to organs such as the heart, kidneys, and liver.

Hair loss is the most common visible side effect. The cells in hair follicles reproduce rapidly, and cancer drugs

Chemotherapy drugs impair cell division in the area of the cancer tumor, thus stopping the spread of the cancer.

Unfortunately, scientists have not found any one single drug that can attack and destroy cancerous cells. Scientists do have a number of drugs that work on specific parts of the problem. Many chemotherapy strategies involve using a number of different chemotherapy drugs together.

Drugs are sometimes used with another treatment called radiation therapy. This involves firing a beam of atomic particles at the atoms that make up the biological structure of the cancerous cell. The abnormal cell dies, and the tumor gets smaller. These cancer-fighting treatments are often very successful.

A wide variety of chemotherapy drug groups is in use and scientists are working to produce more. Examples of these drugs are mitomycin C ($C_{15}H_{18}N_4O_5$), cisplatin ($C_{12}H_6N_2Pt$), and melphalan ($C_{13}H_{18}Cl_2N_2O_2$). Many

Fluorouracil is a chemotherapy drug that is used for treating cancer of the colon.

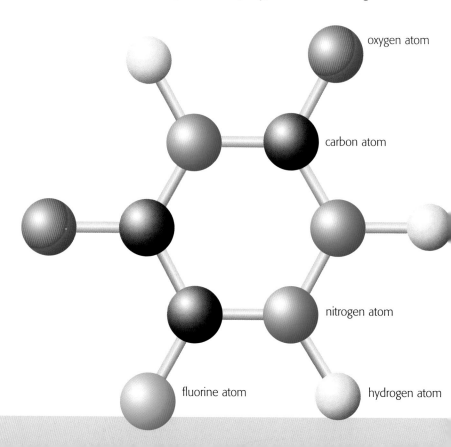

oxygen atom

carbon atom

nitrogen atom

fluorine atom

hydrogen atom

Chemistry in Action

Bacterial cancer treatment

Sometimes, it is difficult to get chemotherapy drugs into cancer tumors. One experimental approach is to use biologically engineered bacteria to produce and deliver the drugs. The bacteria used are anaerobic (they do not need oxygen to live). They are injected directly into the cancerous growth where they thrive and multiply. As they grow, the bacteria release chemotherapy drugs into the cancerous cells.

attack rapidly reproducing cells. Thus, they attack the cells of hair follicles.

Some chemotherapy treatments combine a number of drugs or use several different drugs in a rapid succession. Other treatments are designed to shrink or slow the growth of cancerous cells to remove them before surgery. Sometimes, treatments start after surgery to keep the cancer from reappearing. In some situations, it may not be possible to completely remove the cancerous cells. Then, chemotherapy drugs are given to slow the cancer growth and increase the life expectancy of the patient. Considerable amounts of money are spent on cancer research. Scientists hope eventually to find new chemotherapy treatments that will cure all kinds of cancers.

▶ *One procedure physicians can use to view the intestines is the barium enema. This involves filling the large intestine with barium sulfate (blue), then making an X-ray image. The yellow areas on this image show a condition called diverticulosis.*

MEDICAL IMAGING

Medical imaging is the use of noninvasive techniques that allow a physician to see into the body. Using these techniques, physicians can identify problems such as broken bones, internal bleeding, or see where cancer tumors are growing.

Radiography or X-ray imaging is one of the oldest forms of medical imaging. In the late-19th century, Wilhelm Röntgen (1845–1923) discovered this procedure could form an image of bones. X-rays are produced by firing a stream of electrons (negatively charged atomic particles) at the metal tungsten. When the electrons hit the tungsten atoms, an electron from deep inside the atom is knocked away,

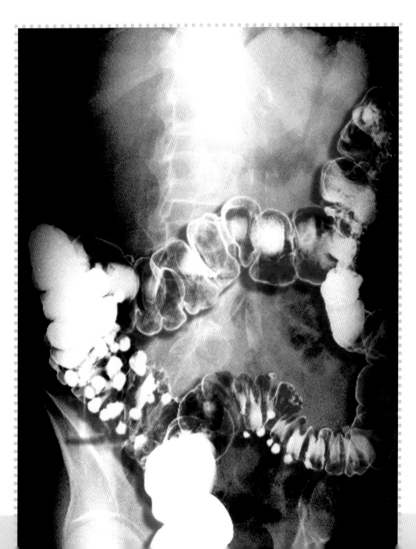

and another electron drops into its place. This produces waves of X-rays, which can pass through soft materials but are reflected off bone. The image of the bone can be captured on photographic film and developed into an image.

By examining an X-ray image, a physician can identify broken bones. Because X-rays pass through the soft tissues of the body, they do not make

▷ *A magnetic resonance image of a child's knee. The light blue areas are bone, and the brown regions are muscles.*

▽ *Serious fracturing of a man's skull is visible in this 3-D computed tomography image.*

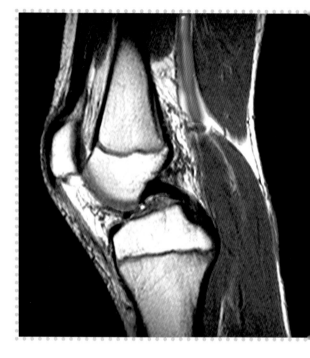

an image of them. However, if an internal organ is filled with a liquid that keeps the X-rays from passing through, a physician can make an examination. The liquid used is usually barium sulfate ($BaSO_4$) or an iodine compound. The procedure is used to produce images of blood vessels or part of the digestive tract.

X-rays may also be used to identify problems such as pneumonia, lung cancer, pulmonary edema, or kidney stones. The X-ray procedure is easy and inexpensive, but there are other medical imaging technologies.

A similar technique is the computed tomography (CT) scan. This technique also uses

Chemistry in Action

Forensic chemistry

Forensic chemistry, and its role in solving crimes, has been featured in numerous movies and television shows. Forensic chemists spend much of their time in laboratories, performing tests. They use a variety of hi-tech instruments to identify chemicals. Forensic experts also use techniques such as polymerase chain reactions (PCR; *see* vol. 9: p. 63) to copy DNA to make DNA fingerprints. The information forensic chemists provide to investigators is often extremely useful. While a career in forensic chemistry may not be as glamorous as portrayed in the movies, it is still very rewarding. And it allows the chemist to use the latest technology to solve crimes.

▶ *A police forensic officer examines a gun. Molecules of the gun's scent are captured by the odor detector, which the officer is holding. The molecules can then be sent for chemical analysis.*

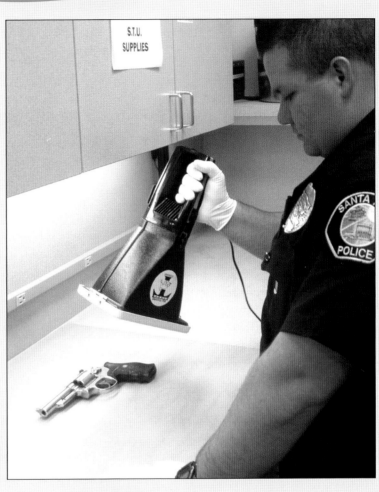

X-rays to create images of thin slices of part of the body. These thin slices can then be put together in a computer to create a 3-D image. This provides physicians with a much better view than an X-ray image.

Magnetic resonance imaging (MRI) is a powerful medical imaging tool because it helps physicians get a 3-D view of the inside of the body. It uses very strong magnetic fields to make

hydrogen atoms absorb microwave radiation at particular wavelengths. An image is created by measuring how much radiation has been absorbed. The advantage of MRI is that it only detects hydrogen in soft tissues and not bones. This means that the resulting image shows only what is happening in the soft tissues. With a computer, the images from the MRI can be joined together to create a 3-D image of the soft tissues.

See also ...
• *Metabolic Pathways, Vol. 9: pp. 30–45.*

More Information

BOOKS

Atkins, P. W. *The Periodic Kingdom: A Journey into the Land of Chemical Elements.* New York, NY: Basic Books, 1997.

Bendick, J., and Wiker, B. *The Mystery of the Periodic Table (Living History Library).* Bathgate, ND: Bethlehem Books, 2003.

Berg, J., Stryer, L., and Tymoczko, J. *Biochemistry.* New York, NY: W. H. Freeman, 2002.

Brown, T., Burdge, J., Bursten, B., and LeMay, E. *Chemistry: The Central Science.* 10th ed. Englewood Cliffs, NJ: Prentice Hall, 2005.

Cobb, C., and Fetterolf, M. L. *The Joy of Chemistry: The Amazing Science of Familiar Things.* Amherst, NY: Prometheus Books, 2005.

Cox, M., and Nelson, D. *Lehninger's Principles of Biochemistry.* 4th ed. New York, NY: W. H. Freeman, 2004.

Davis, M. *Modern Chemistry.* New York, NY: Henry Holt, 2000.

Herr, N., and Cunningham, J. *Hands-on Chemistry Activities with Real Life Applications.* Hoboken, NJ: Jossey-Bass, 2002.

Houck, Clifford C., and Post, Richard. *Chemistry: Concepts and Problems.* Hoboken, NJ: Wiley, 1996.

Karukstis, K. K., and Van Hecke, G. R. *Chemistry Connections: The Chemical Basis of Everyday Phenomena.* Burlington, MA: Academic Press, 2003.

LeMay, E. *Chemistry: Connections to Our Changing World.* New York, NY: Prentice Hall (Pearson Education), 2000.

Oxlade, C. *Elements and Compounds.* Chicago, IL: Heinemann, 2002.

Poynter, M. *Marie Curie: Discoverer of Radium (Great Minds of Science).* Berkeley Heights, NJ: Enslow Publishers, 2007.

Saunders, N. *Fluorine and the Halogens.* Chicago, IL: Heinemann Library, 2005.

Shevick, E., and Wheeler, R. *Great Scientists in Action: Early Life, Discoveries, and Experiments.* Carthage, IL: Teaching and Learning Company, 2004.

Stwertka, A. *A Guide to the Elements.* New York, NY: Oxford University Press, 2002.

Tiner, J. H. *Exploring the World of Chemistry: From Ancient Metals to High-Speed Computers.* Green Forest, AZ: Master Books, 2000.

Trombley, L., and Williams, F. *Mastering the Periodic Table: 50 Activities on the Elements.* Portland, ME: Walch, 2002.

Walker, P., and Wood, E. *Crime Scene Investigations: Real-life Science Labs for Grades 6–12.* Hoboken, NJ: Jossey-Bass, 2002.

Wertheim, J. *Illustrated Dictionary of Chemistry (Usborne Illustrated Dictionaries).* Tulsa, OK: Usborne Publishing, 2000.

Wilbraham, A., et al. *Chemistry.* New York, NY: Prentice Hall (Pearson Education), 2000.

Woodford, C., and Clowes, M. *Routes of Science: Atoms and Molecules.* San Diego, CA: Blackbirch Press, 2004.

WEB SITES

The Art and Science of Bubbles
www.sdahq.org/sdakids/bubbles
*Information and activities
about bubbles.*

Chemical Achievers
www.chemheritage.org/classroom/
chemach/index.html
*Biographical details about leading
chemists and their discoveries.*

The Chemistry of Batteries
www.science.uwaterloo.ca/~cchieh/
cact/c123/battery.html
Explanation of how batteries work.

The Chemistry of Chilli Peppers
www.chemsoc.org/exemplarchem/
entries/mbellringer
*Fun site giving information on the
chemistry of chilli peppers.*

The Chemistry of Fireworks
library.thinkquest.org/15384/
chem/chem.htm
*Information on the chemical
reactions that occur when
a firework explodes.*

The Chemistry of Water
www.biology.arizona.edu/
biochemistry/tutorials/chemistry/
page3.html
*Chemistry of water and other
aspects of biochemistry.*

Chemistry: The Periodic Table Online
www.webelements.com
Detailed information about elements.

Chemistry Tutor
library.thinkquest.org/2923
*A series of Web pages that help
with chemistry assignments.*

Chem4Kids
www.chem4Kids.com
*Includes sections on matter, atoms,
elements, and biochemistry.*

Chemtutor Elements
www.chemtutor.com/elem.htm
*Information on a selection of
the elements.*

Eric Weisstein's World of Chemistry
scienceworld.wolfram.com/
chemistry
*Chemistry information divided into
eight broad topics, from chemical
reactions to quantum chemistry.*

General Chemistry Help
chemed.chem.purdue.edu/genchem
*General information on chemistry
plus movie clips of key concepts.*

Molecular Models
chemlabs.uoregon.edu/
GeneralResources/models/
models.html
*A site that explains the use
of molecular models.*

New Scientist
www.newscientist.com/home.ns
*Online science magazine providing
general news on scientific
developments.*

Periodic Tables
www.chemistrycoach.com/periodic_
tables.htm#Periodic%20Tables
*A list of links to sites that have
information on the periodic table.*

The Physical Properties of Minerals
mineral.galleries.com/minerals/
physical.htm
Methods for identifying minerals.

**Understanding Our Planet Through
Chemistry**
minerals.cr.usgs.gov/gips/
aii-home.htm
*Site that shows how chemists
and geologists use analytical
chemistry to study Earth.*

Scientific American
www.sciam.com
*Latest news on developments
in science and technology.*

Snowflakes and Snow Crystals
www.its.caltech.edu/~atomic/
snowcrystals
*A guide to snowflakes, snow
crystals, and other ice
phenomena.*

Virtual Laboratory: Ideal Gas Laws
zebu.uoregon.edu/nsf/piston.html
*University of Oregon site showing
simulation of ideal gas laws.*

What Is Salt?
www.saltinstitute.org/15.html
Information on common salt.

Periodic Table

The periodic table organizes all the chemical elements into a simple chart according to the physical and chemical properties of their atoms. The elements are arranged by atomic number from 1 to 116. The atomic number is based on the number of protons in the nucleus of the atom. The atomic mass is the combined mass of protons and neutrons in the nucleus. Each element has a chemical symbol that is an abbreviation of its name. In some cases, such as potassium,

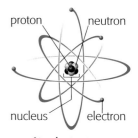

Atomic structure

33	Atomic (proton) number
As	Chemical symbol
Arsenic	Element name
75	Atomic mass

☐ HYDROGEN
▨ ALKALI METALS
▨ ALKALINE-EARTH METALS
☐ METALS
▨ LANTHANIDES

	Group 1	**Group 2**	**Group 3**	**Group 4**	**Group 5**	**Group 6**	**Group 7**	**Group 8**	**Group 9**
Period 1	1 **H** Hydrogen 1								
Period 2	3 **Li** Lithium 7	4 **Be** Beryllium 9							
Period 3	11 **Na** Sodium 23	12 **Mg** Magnesium 24							
Period 4	19 **K** Potassium 39	20 **Ca** Calcium 40	21 **Sc** Scandium 45	22 **Ti** Titanium 48	23 **V** Vanadium 51	24 **Cr** Chromium 52	25 **Mn** Manganese 55	26 **Fe** Iron 56	27 **Co** Cobalt 59
Period 5	37 **Rb** Rubidium 85	38 **Sr** Strontium 88	39 **Y** Yttrium 89	40 **Zr** Zirconium 91	41 **Nb** Niobium 93	42 **Mo** Molybdenum 96	43 **Tc** Technetium (98)	44 **Ru** Ruthenium 101	45 **Rh** Rhodium 103
Period 6	55 **Cs** Cesium 133	56 **Ba** Barium 137	Lanthanides	72 **Hf** Hafnium 179	73 **Ta** Tantalum 181	74 **W** Tungsten 184	75 **Re** Rhenium 186	76 **Os** Osmium 190	77 **Ir** Iridium 192
Period 7	87 **Fr** Francium 223	88 **Ra** Radium 226	Actinides	104 **Rf** Rutherfordium (263)	105 **Db** Dubnium (268)	106 **Sg** Seaborgium (266)	107 **Bh** Bohrium (272)	108 **Hs** Hassium (277)	109 **Mt** Meitnerium (276)

Transition metals

rare-earth elements ⎡ **Lanthanides**
              ⎣ **Actinides**

57 **La** Lanthanum 39	58 **Ce** Cerium 140	59 **Pr** Praseodymium 141	60 **Nd** Neodymium 144	61 **Pm** Promethium (145)
89 **Ac** Actinium 227	90 **Th** Thorium 232	91 **Pa** Protactinium 231	92 **U** Uranium 238	93 **Np** Neptunium (237)

the symbol is an abbreviation of its Latin name ("K" stands for *kalium*). The name by which the element is commonly known is given in full underneath the symbol. The last item in the element box is the atomic mass. This is the average mass of an atom of the element.

Scientists have arranged the elements into vertical columns called groups and horizontal rows called periods. Elements in any one group all have the same number of electrons in their outer shell and have similar chemical properties. Periods represent the increasing number of electrons it takes to fill the inner and outer shells and become stable. When all the spaces have been filled (Group 18 atoms have all their shells filled) the next period begins. Further explanation of the periodic table is given in Volume 5.

ACTINIDES

NOBLE GASES

NONMETALS

METALLOIDS

Group 18

			Group 13	Group 14	Group 15	Group 16	Group 17	2 **He** Helium 4
			5 **B** Boron 11	6 **C** Carbon 12	7 **N** Nitrogen 14	8 **O** Oxygen 16	9 **F** Fluorine 19	10 **Ne** Neon 20
Group 10	Group 11	Group 12	13 **Al** Aluminum 27	14 **Si** Silicon 28	15 **P** Phosphorus 31	16 **S** Sulfur 32	17 **Cl** Chlorine 35	18 **Ar** Argon 40
28 **Ni** Nickel 59	29 **Cu** Copper 64	30 **Zn** Zinc 65	31 **Ga** Gallium 70	32 **Ge** Germanium 73	33 **As** Arsenic 75	34 **Se** Selenium 79	35 **Br** Bromine 80	36 **Kr** Krypton 84
46 **Pd** Palladium 106	47 **Ag** Silver 108	48 **Cd** Cadmium 112	49 **In** Indium 115	50 **Sn** Tin 119	51 **Sb** Antimony 122	52 **Te** Tellurium 128	53 **I** Iodine 127	54 **Xe** Xenon 131
78 **Pt** Platinum 195	79 **Au** Gold 197	80 **Hg** Mercury 201	81 **Tl** Thallium 204	82 **Pb** Lead 207	83 **Bi** Bismuth 209	84 **Po** Polonium (209)	85 **At** Astatine (210)	84 **Rn** Radon (222)
110 **Ds** Darmstadtium (281)	111 **Rg** Roentgenium (280)	112 **Uub** Ununbium (285)	113 **Uut** Ununtrium (284)	114 **Uuq** Ununquadium (289)	115 **Uup** Ununpentium (288)	116 **Uuh** Ununhexium (292)		

artificial elements

62 **Sm** Samarium 150	63 **Eu** Europium 152	64 **Gd** Gadolinium 157	65 **Tb** Terbium 159	66 **Dy** Dysprosium 163	67 **Ho** Holmium 165	68 **Er** Erbium 167	69 **Tm** Thulium 169	70 **Yb** Ytterbium 173	71 **Lu** Lutetium 175
94 **Pu** Plutonium (244)	95 **Am** Americium (243)	96 **Cm** Curium (247)	97 **Bk** Berkelium (247)	98 **Cf** Californium (251)	99 **Es** Einsteinium (252)	100 **Fm** Fermium (257)	101 **Md** Mendelevium (258)	102 **No** Nobelium (259)	103 **Lr** Lawrencium (260)

Glossary

acid Substance that dissolves in water to form hydrogen ions (H^+). Acids are neutralized by alkalis and have a pH below 7.

acid rain Rain that has an unusually high level of acidity resulting from pollution. Acid rain causes damage to forests, lakes, rivers, and buildings.

adsorption The process of molecules becoming attached to a surface.

alkali Substance that dissolves in water to form hydroxide ions (OH^-). Alkalis have a pH greater than 7 and react with acids to form salts.

allotrope A different form of the same element in which the atoms are arranged in a different structure.

alloy A metallic substance that contains two or more metals. An alloy may also be made of a metal and a small amount of a nonmetal. Steel, for example, is an alloy of iron and carbon.

atom The smallest independent building block of matter. All substances are made of atoms.

atomic mass The number of protons and neutrons in an atom's nucleus.

atomic number The number of protons in a nucleus.

bond A chemical connection between atoms.

catalyst Substance that speeds up a chemical reaction but is left unchanged at the end of the reaction.

chemical equation Symbols and numbers that show how reactants change into products during a chemical reaction.

chemical formula The letters and numbers that represent a chemical compound, such as "H_2O" for water.

chemical symbol The letters that represent a chemical, such as "Cl" for chlorine or "Na" for sodium.

combustion The reaction that causes burning. Combustion is generally a reaction with oxygen in the air.

compound Substance made from more than one element and that has undergone a chemical reaction.

condensation The change of state from a gas to a liquid.

condensation reaction A reaction that produces water.

conductor A substance that carries electricity and heat.

contact process Industrial process for producing sulfuric acid.

corrosion The slow wearing away of metals or solids by chemical attack.

covalent bond Bond in which atoms share one or more electrons.

cracking Process by which products of fractional distillation are broken down into simpler hydrocarbons.

crosslink A bond between two polymers.

crystal A solid made of regular repeating patterns of atoms.

density The mass of substance in a unit of volume.

deposit A mineral vein or ore inside another rock.

dipole attraction The attractive force between the electrically charged ends of molecules.

dissolve To form a solution.

distillation The process of evaporation and condensation used to separate a mixture of liquids according to their boiling points. Also a method of purifying a liquid.

electrolyte Liquid containing ions that carries a current between electrodes.

electromagnetic radiation Energy emitted by a source in the form of gamma rays, X-rays, ultraviolet light, visible light, infrared, microwaves, or radio waves.

electromagnetic spectrum The range of energy waves that includes visible light, infrared, and radio waves.

electron A tiny negatively charged particle that moves around the nucleus of an atom.

element A material that cannot be broken up into simpler ingredients. Elements contain only one type of atom.

enzyme A biological protein that acts as a catalyst.

erosion The removal and transport of small pieces of rock by wind, water, or ice.

evaporation The change of state from a liquid to a gas when the liquid is at a temperature below its boiling point.

fermentation A reaction in which sugar is turned into ethanol.

fission Process by which a large atom breaks up into two or more smaller fragments.

fossil fuels Fuels formed from organic matter through a long process of heating and compression.

fractional distillation The process of heating crude oil to separate different hydrocarbon components.

Frasch process Industrial process for extracting raw sulfur from underground deposits.

functional group A section of an organic molecule that gives it certain chemical properties.

fusion When two small atoms fuse to make a single larger atom.

geologist Scientist who studies rocks and minerals.

group A column of related elements in the periodic table.

greenhouse gases Gases such as carbon dioxide and methane that trap heat in Earth's atmosphere.

Haber process Industrial process for producing ammonia.

insulator A substance that does not transfer an electric current or heat.

ion An atom that has lost or gained one or more electrons.

ionic bond Bond in which one atom gives one or more electrons to another atom.

ionization The formation of ions by adding or removing electrons from atoms.

isotope Atoms of a given element always have the same number of protons but can have different numbers of neutrons. These different versions of the same element are called isotopes.

lubricant A substance that helps surfaces slide past each other.

matter Anything that can be weighed.

metal An element that is usually solid, shiny, malleable, ductile, and conductive.

metallic bond Bond in which outer electrons are free to move in the spaces between the atoms.

metalloid Elements that have properties of both metals and nonmetals.

metallurgy The science and technology of metals, including methods of extraction and use.

mineral A naturally occurring compound, such as those that make up rocks and soil.

mole The amount of any substance that contains the same number of atoms as in 12 grams of carbon-12 atoms. This number is 6.022×10^{23}.

molecule Two or more joined atoms that have a unique shape and size.

neutron One of the particles that make up the nucleus of an atom. Neutrons do not have an electric charge.

noble gases A group of gases that rarely react with other elements.

nonmetal Any element that is not a metal. Most nonmetals are gases, such as hydrogen and argon.

nonrenewable energy Sources of energy such as oil and coal and other fossil fuels that will eventually run out and cannot be replaced.

nucleus The central part of an atom. The nucleus contains protons and neutrons. The exception is hydrogen, which contains only one proton.

ore A mineral that contains valuable amounts of materials such as copper, sulfur, or tin.

organic A compound that is made of carbon and hydrogen.

oxidation The addition of oxygen to a compound. Also the loss of electrons from an atom.

oxidation state A number used to describe how many electrons an atom can lose or gain.

oxide A compound that contains oxygen.

ozone A form of oxygen in which three oxygen atoms join to form a molecule.

period A row of elements across the periodic table.

petrochemicals Organic chemicals that are made from petroleum or natural gas.

pH A measure of acidity and alkalinity.

phase change A change from one state to another.

photon A particle that carries a quantity of energy, such as in the form of light.

photosynthesis A chemical reaction in which plants use energy from the sun to change carbon dioxide and water into food.

plastic An organic polymer that can be molded or shaped into objects for films by heat.

polymerization The process that makes short chains (monomers) of organic molecules join together to make polymers.

polysaccharide Carbohydrate made of many saccharide molecules.

pressure The force produced by pressing on something.

product The new substance or substances created by a chemical reaction.

proton A positively charged particle found in an atom's nucleus.

radioactive decay Process in which small particles break off from an unstable nucleus. These are alpha particles (helium nuclei), beta particles (electrons), or gamma rays (a form of electromagnetic radiation).

radiation The products of radioactivity—alpha and beta particles and gamma rays.

reactants The ingredients necessary for a chemical reaction.

refining The process of extracting important minerals from ores.

relative atomic mass A measure of the mass of an atom compared with the mass of another atom. The values used are the same as those for atomic mass.

relative molecular mass The sum of all the atomic masses of the atoms in a molecule.

renewable energy Unlimited sources of energy such as the Sun and wind.

salt A compound made from positive and negative ions that forms when an alkali reacts with an acid.

seismic survey A method of determining the structure of underground rock formations by measuring the vibrations produced by test explosions.

smelting Method for purifying metal from their ores.

solute A substance that dissolves in a solvent.

solution A mixture of two or more elements or compounds in a single state (solid, liquid, or gas).

Solvay process Industrial process for producing sodium carbonate.

solvent The liquid that dissolves a solute.

temperature A measure of how fast molecules are moving.

van der Waals forces Short-lived forces between atoms and molecules.

viscous Describes a liquid that is not very runny and flows slowly.

volatile Describes a liquid that evaporates easily.

weathering The processes that break rocks into smaller parts. Weathering may be mechanical, resulting from physical forces such as abrasion by ice and wind, or chemical, such as the dissolving of chemicals in rocks by water.

Index